SENSIBLE SHARE INVESTING

Austin Donnelly

Best wishes, Prof Richard Thaler

Austin Donnelly.

Oct 20 1995.

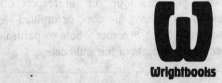

Wrightbooks

First published in 1995
Wrightbooks Pty Ltd
PO Box 2301
North Brighton
Victoria 3186

ACN 007 050 277

Ph: (03) 596 4262
Fax: (03) 596 4206

National Library of Australia
Cataloguing-in-publication data:

Donnelly, Austin
  Sensible share investing: better results through careful timing.
  Includes index.
  ISBN 1 875857 03 6
  1. Stocks. 2. Stocks - Australia. I. Title.
332.6322

Cover design by Rob Cowpe
Printed in Australia by McPherson's Printing Group
ISBN: 1 875857 03 6

Acknowledgements

As this book is based on 40 years experience in the investment business, there are many people whose influence has had a bearing on the development of my thinking on *Sensible Share Investing*. My first thanks should go to the thousands of clients with whom I have dealt over the years. Helping them see the realities of investment markets more clearly has inevitably clarified my thinking on many of the principles involved.

Like any person devoted to portraying the reality of share markets as distinct from the fables, fallacies and folklore of the conventional investment wisdom, I have been encouraged by the achievements of Warren Buffett of Berkshire Hathaway in Omaha Nebraska, USA, probably the most successful investor in the world. His outstanding success has demonstrated that the path to share investing success is not made up of uncritical acceptance of the conventional investment wisdom.

Nor is it in following market hype or elegant but impractical theories such as the efficient market hypothesis. The main lesson from a study of his achievements is that success lies in logic common sense and discipline, with a willingness to learn from the lessons of the past — all qualities which are fairly rare in many investment institutions.

I appreciate the benefits I have gained from the writings, some of which are quoted in the book, of John Bogle of the Vanguard Investment Group, of Valley Forge, PA, USA, George Soros of the Soros Foundations, New York and the American Association of Independent Investors, of Chicago.

Shashanna Kocinski, of Behavioural Insights Pty. Ltd., City of the Gold Coast, Queensland has been very helpful with advice on how modern professional psychological studies into the behaviour of groups explains much of the way in which share markets can be affected by what non-psychologists may call the herd instinct and mob psychology.

The contents of this book, as with the other 40 which I have written, have been improved greatly by many suggestions from my wife, Sheila. Her thorough work in proof-reading and in suggesting where the wording needed to be clarified should make it an easier book to read. For this I am deeply grateful.

To my secretary, Yvonne Ware, go my thanks for dedication and patience in typing the drafts and for general assistance on the project.

To my daughter Melda Donnelly

and my Son-in-law Ian Murdoch

In appreciation of their involvement in carrying on the investment advisory, financial planning and newsletter publishing company, Donnelly Money Management Pty Ltd which I founded many years ago.

In the afternoon of my life it is encouraging to be associated with them. It is very comforting to me to know, that in the prime of their lives, they are devoted to carrying on the standards of objective unbiased advice which I have constantly striven to maintain over the last 40 years.

Contents

Contents (Cont'd)

Chapter 1

For Successful Share
Investing Medium Term
Timing is the Name
of the Game

The lessons of history — vastly different results

We are constantly told by many fund managers, advisers and
the financial media that in share investing timing does not
matter. Why, then, was there such a marked difference in the
medium term results of two groups of share investors who
invested at different times?

Group A — an average of 22.4 per cent per annum compound
Group B — an average of 4.5 per cent per annum compound.

Why was the downside risk of the two groups so different?

Group A — the worst result a *profit* of 10.7 per cent per
annum
Group B — the worst result a *loss* of 9.21 per cent per
annum.

As that latter figure is an annual figure the total loss over a
five year period works out at *38 per cent*.

Unit trusts and managed funds — Why is it that the
institutions which manage unit trusts, superannuation funds,
rollover products and the like, who claim special expertise,
have generally been unable to do as well as the market
average?

The answer: medium term timing

The answer to those questions is medium term timing. The
investors in Group A achieved far better results than was
achieved by investors in Group B, and the fund managers,

because they invested when share prices, on objective standards, were low. On the basis of past experience, there was a high probability of good returns and low downside risk of loss for investments made at these low prices.

By contrast, the investors in group B invested when, by objective standards, share prices were dangerously high. Past experience showed that at those high price levels, good returns were unlikely and there was a significant downside risk of serious loss.

To put it another way, Group A invested when share prices were in Zone 5, the most favourable zone in the ranking system I have developed as the result of very close study of share market behaviour during my 40 years experience in the investment business.

The zone system ranging from Zone 5, the most *favourable* for share investing, to Zone 1, the most *unfavourable,* is based on objective standards, namely dividend yield at time of investing and prices related to the long term trend. It is based on research into our database which goes back to 1960. It is not put forward as infallible or as a get-rich-quick scheme. But it is a far more practicable approach than other investment approaches for investors who seek better results with lower downside risk.

My research into the US and British markets shows broadly similar patterns for the zone system in those markets. The importance of average market dividend yield at time of investment in the US market has also been pointed out in the comment by the eminent American investment specialist John Bogle which is quoted on page 15.

Conventional investment wisdom — fables and fallacies

Many experienced share investors may initially find the above comments hard to accept, because they differ so much from the conventional investment wisdom and from what they are told in prospectuses and media comments.

This reflects one important point which share investors and investors of all kinds must remember. It is the need to be wary of the RCs — not the Roman Catholics but the **Risk**

Concealers. Risk concealing is very profitable for many people in the investment business because it keeps them in the manner to which they have become accustomed.

Sometimes it is the result of a more or less accidental process of what I call **Goebbeling.** Named after Josef Goebbels the Nazi Propaganda Minister, it is the process by which untrue statements, which if repeated for long enough, tend to be accepted as true. Whether the risk concealing is deliberate or accidental, it can be very bad news for the investing public who are the victims of the process.

So, share investors need to know whether, on the basis of their ability to cope with the risk of the large capital losses, it is wise at various times to increase or reduce their investments in shares. Apart from policy considerations relating to individual situations (e.g. amount of capital available for investing, income from other sources and so on), there are a number of objective standards to assist in timing decisions.

The crucial importance of timing

From the figures quoted in the opening paragraphs it is obvious that timing is crucial to success in share investing. This does not mean that you should engage in a futile quest to predict the precise level at which the share market reaches the peak of a boom or the trough of a slump.

Share investment results, however, will be a good deal better if you achieve even moderate success in recognising that timing is important and by *increasing* share investment when the market is in the lower phase of the cycle and *reducing* it when booms have taken prices up to dangerously high levels at which the almost inevitable slump could be imminent.

The timing process which is discussed at length later in the book is facilitated by these factors:

➤ **The use of proven indicators** such as average dividend yield, share prices in relation to their long term trend and the ratio of total market capitalisation of listed shares to gross domestic product.

➤ **Avoiding the risk of one incorrect decision** causing serious trouble by moving gradually in the step system. For example, if selling is necessary, initially sell a portion of planned sales. Then watch the market closely for the timing of further sales.

Proof of the pudding — protective action before slumps

It was the awareness of timing indicators described above which made it possible for me to be one of the few advisers who warned of the 1987 stock market crash — in the August 1987 issue of my newsletter, in comments published in 12 newspapers including on the front page of the *Herald* in Melbourne, and in an ABC Radio interview the day before the crash. (The *Investor Alert* of the Australian Investors Association, which I wrote in November 1993 two months before the 1994 slump started, warned that a slump could be imminent and was also based on those principles.)

Precautionary selling action based on those timing indicators enabled investors to preserve profits, to protect capital from erosion in the slump and to have funds available for investment at better prices in the downturn.

Practical rather than conventional analysis

Though timing is important in share investing, it is not the only consideration. There is a need for practical, down-to-earth analysis of trends in the economy and in earnings of the corporate sector — as distinct from conventional analysis.

(Later chapters explain the importance of going beyond conventional analysis to more significant items such as the rate of return on net equity. Another important step is the further analysis of earnings into components from business operations, from gearing benefits and tax benefits.)

The evolution of investment theory and practice

The evolution of investment theory and practice during the last 50 or so years is summarised briefly below. There are other more detailed references to some of the concepts later in this book.

◆ *Buy and hold — the Bo Peep approach*

Fifty years ago, investing in stocks was seen almost exclusively as buying stocks in well known well established companies and putting them in the "old oak chest ". This was very passive investment with the investor leaving the stocks alone. Investors believed in a paraphrase of the words of the nursery rhyme, "Little Bo Peep", namely, leave them alone and they will come home bringing their capital gains behind them.

◆ *Fundamental analysis and intrinsic value*

Benjamin Graham, known as the father of security analysis, and his colleagues developed the first disciplined approach to security analysis. The book, *Security Analysis,* by Graham, Dodd and Cottle was the text book on which most investment education was based for many years. The latest book which revises and updates that concept is entitled, *Graham and Dodd's Security Analysis* by Sydney Cottle, Roger F. Murray and Frank E. Block (McGraw Hill, New York, 5th Edition 1988).

Warren Buffett of Omaha, Nebraska, whose performance record is generally considered to be the best in the US (and possibly the world) over the last 30 years or so attributes part of his success to applying the principles espoused by Ben Graham.

Those principles are related to the means of finding undervalued stocks with a current price below their *intrinsic value*. The intrinsic value is based on finding:

➣ the present value of the stream of dividends based on current dividend per stock

➣ estimated rate of growth in dividends

➣ an appropriate required rate of return to allow for the risk involved in stock investments.

The Graham approach considers trends in the economy, the corporate sector, industry and the company to estimate earnings per share at a future date. Multiplying that figure by an appropriate estimated price earnings multiple gives an estimated value for the share at a future date. Discounting that figure to the present by using present value techniques gives an estimated intrinsic value. In essence, if the current market price were below that figure then it was a possible buy.

Other useful concepts developed by Ben Graham included seeking stocks with a current market price below book value.

◆ *Technical analysis*

Technical analysts, sometimes called chartists, believe that rather than use fundamental analysis, a better idea of future stock price changes and hence of profitable opportunities can be found in a study of the market movements by using charts of stock prices and volume. Essentially, technical analysis is based on a study of patterns on charts, as well as price trends, and support and resistance levels at which rising or falling trends may be halted or reversed.

◆ *The capital asset pricing model*

Over the last 20 years or so, there was great growth in the number of finance departments at Universities teaching and researching market behaviour. So it is not surprising that a more rigorous approach emerged.

To oversimplify in the interests of brevity, the capital asset pricing model assumes that investors make rational investment decisions and that they are averse to risk — so that they would demand higher returns for accepting greater risk. It also assumes that the volatility of variations of returns is a measure of risk.

One of the concepts flowing from the capital asset pricing model is what is called the *beta* which measures the risk of a stock related to the market average. Over a period, a stock with a beta of 2 would move up or down twice as much as the appropriate market average, for example the All Ordinaries Index. A beta of 0.5 indicates that the stock would move up or down half as much as the market average. If the beta is 1, the stock should move up or down at the same rate as the market.

The beta of a portfolio is the weighted average of the betas of the individual stocks in the portfolio.

The return on the share market is seen as comprising the risk free rate of return, generally the return on short term Treasury Bonds, plus a premium to allow for the greater risk of stocks. For an individual stock, the return should be the average market return multiplied by the beta for the stock. There is also another component generally called *alpha* which could be positive or negative. This component includes random and unexplained factors not accounted for by the other components

◆ *The efficient market hypothesis*

More or less associated with the capital asset pricing model is the efficient market hypothesis. In an abbreviated and simplified description this hypothesis states that, as all significant information about listed companies is widely publicised, it is quickly reflected in stock prices. Hence, it argues, the current price of any stock and the overall position of the market is the best unbiased estimate of what they should be. So, it asserts, it is not worthwhile to try to select stocks or to time moves into or out of the stock market.

One manifestation of belief in this hypothesis was the development of indexed stock funds. These funds try as closely as possible to replicate the performance of the market by keeping the portfolio in line with the relevant market index.

◆ *Asset allocation and buy and hold*

A more recent development is the concept of allocating proportions of capital to various types of investments such as stocks, fixed-interest investments and cash, e.g. cash management trusts and very short term deposits. The proportion allocated to each segment would depend on such factors as the need for definite assured investment income and freedom from large capital fluctuations.

On periodical reviews, the portfolios are rebalanced to the original asset allocation mix, but the allocation once set is considered as permanent. This approach is basically the approach suggested in educational programmes of the American Association of Independent Investors, an organisation with 170,000 members.

◆ *Behavioural finance*

This more recent development is discussed in *Advances In Behavioural Finance,* Richard H. Thaler Ed, (Russell Sage Foundation, New York, 1993), which is a collection of papers on the subject. In the introduction, Professor Thaler states at page xvii.

> *"The common thread in these papers is the combination of a concern with real world problems and a willingness to consider all explanations in the search for understanding. I think of behavioural finance as simply 'open minded finance'. Sometimes in order to find the solution to an empirical puzzle, it is necessary to entertain the possibility that some of the agents in the economy behave less than fully rationally some of the time."*

To put it another way, the behavioural finance approach to stock market behaviour is based on the reality that often most people do not think and act as economists think and act. The papers include references to the effect of fads and fashions on stock markets and the tendency for specialists in making comments or predictions to, at least subconsciously, try to ensure that they are not too far away from the consensus.

How experience shows defects in various approaches

◆ *Buy and hold*

In the post war period up to about 1965, the buy-and-hold philosophy worked well because there was a firm long term upward trend, associated with the prosperity of the post-War expansion and the first entry into the share market of institutions such as life insurance companies, as significant investors. In those times, most stocks could be bought to provide an initial dividend yield above the fixed interest rate. So they started off well ahead in contrast to later years when booms pushed prices up to levels at which the average dividend yield was way below the return available from interest rates on other investments.

Moreover, there have been periods during which the All Ordinaries has shown no sustained gain. The longest was 15 years from 1959 to 1974. So those conditions do not justify buying and holding which worked well when there was a strong medium term market tide.

◆ *Fundamental analysis and intrinsic value*

To some extent the same matters made the fundamental analysis and intrinsic value approaches invalid. One of the problems was a tendency for analysts to be less than completely objective because of psychological pressures to conform to the conventional wisdom. This led to over-optimistic figures for future growth in earnings and in the price earnings or dividend yields at which stocks would be priced in the future.

Often, there was double counting. Analysts tended to assume that something like the high current price earnings or low dividend yield figures at the top of a boom, which anticipated a rapid growth in earnings, would also apply to the estimated increased future earnings.

◆ *Technical analysis*

Some aspects of the charting approach such as the need for caution about support and resistance levels, and price moves relative to moving averages or trend lines have at times been useful. But technical analysis is based on an illogical belief that past patterns will continue in the future when circumstances may be vastly different. To the best of my knowledge, technical analysis failed to warn of possible major declines in 1987 and at other times.

◆ *Capital asset pricing model*

There are three serious conceptual weaknesses in the capital asset pricing model:

➤ The assumption that investors act rationally is invalid. Human nature being what it is, the actions and decisions of many people are often not rational — that is a reason for wars, bitter family battles and many business failures. They are also affected by fads and the desire to conform.

➤ The assumption that all or most investors are averse to risk is not valid. You cannot be averse to a risk of which you are not aware. Many investors make decisions on the basis of information provided by fund managers or commission-driven advisers which either ignores or plays down risk.

➤ So too is the assumption that the volatility of a stock measured by the standard deviation of returns is a measure of risk. In that measure, favourable and unfavourable deviations from the average are treated similarly. What investors need to know is the maximum loss they may face on the basis of past experience. For example, over a five year period, a capital loss of more than 50 per cent in the share market (even for a well diversified portfolio) compared with a loss of zero on a Treasury Bond with five years to maturity at date of purchase. The number of zigs and zags from the average return is not the crucial point. Using volatility as a measure of risk would produce the misleading result of showing the same degree of risk for one stock, which overall moved up steadily with frequent movements above and below the average, and another which declined sharply with few zigs and zags.

According to the capital asset pricing model, after a sharp decline in the stock market its risk has increased because of increased volatility. But logic would suggest that whatever the risk may have been before the decline, it must be somewhat diminished after the decline when prices are lower.

◆ *The efficient market hypothesis*

This approach is not useful partly because of the weaknesses in the asset pricing model discussed above. The vast difference in results achieved by those who invested in 1982 and sold in 1987 before the crash, compared with those who invested at the peak in 1987 and sold in 1992, shows that the claim that timing does not matter is false. Conceptually, it is flawed as, Professor R. J. Shiller demonstrates in his paper *Stock Prices and Social Dynamics* in Richard H. Thaler Ed *Advances in Behavioural Finance*. He writes (on page 169) that one of the arguments for the efficient market hypothesis *"represents one of the most remarkable errors in the history of economic thought."*

George Soros of the Quantum Fund, who is a very successful investor and trader, is strongly critical of the hypothesis. He makes the point that capital markets are inherently unstable. He writes in *The Alchemy of Finance* (p.301):

> *"Indeed belief in efficient markets renders markets more unstable by short circuiting the corrective processes that would occur if participants recognized that markets are always biased. **The more the theory of efficient markets is believed, the less efficient markets become."** (Emphasis added.)*

From a practical point of view it is not possible to reconcile the efficient market hypothesis with some strange happenings in the stock market. Examples are:

➤ The one day decline of 20 per cent in October 1987

➤ The anomalous January effect and meteoric rises and falls in some stocks such as the example cited by Andrew Tobias which is quoted in Chapter Eighteen.

◆ *Asset allocation and buy and hold*

Part of this approach is a step in the right direction towards recognising the reality of market fluctuations. The re-balancing of portfolios in periodical reviews back to the original asset allocation would mean that after a heavy rise in stock prices, as in 1982 to 1987, some sale of stocks and reinvestment in fixed interest or cash would be necessary. That process would reduce the amount exposed to erosion through the imminent slump. But its weakness is the initial practice of investing the fixed proportion of total assets in stocks even when the market is dangerously overpriced, on the basis of objective indicators such as long term trend and average dividend yield.

This approach suggests that any attempt to time markets should be avoided because it assumes that timing does not work. Its error is in failing to distinguish between short term and medium term market timing. It is true that short term timing does not work. It is not possible to predict with any consistent reliability short term movements.

However, a study of medium term fluctuations over periods such as five years shows a vastly different picture. On certain objective standards, such as average dividend yields or prices related to long term trend, it is possible to determine whether prices are at dangerously high levels. At such levels, experience shows clearly that any new investment in stocks should be deferred and existing investment reduced. Even moderate success in gradually reducing or increasing stock investment on this basis can produce better results than just drifting up and down with the market tide.

◆ *Behavioural Finance*

Of all of the above approaches, the relatively new behavioural finance school is the most helpful to the practical investor in that it focuses on many important matters that other approaches overlook. From an academic viewpoint it may be criticised for not having developed a cohesive general theory. But what investors need today is not elegant theories but an approach that recognises the reality of the market-place.

The capital asset pricing model and the efficient market hypothesis would score well from the viewpoint of being mathematically elegant, formally attractive, and logically consistent. But by not accepting important realities, those theories do not provide the basis of a practical approach to investing in shares. Many investors lost a considerable portion of their capital by investing at highly inflated prices just before the 1987 or other market slumps commenced. If they invested because they accepted the efficient market hypothesis they would find little consolation in the fact that the theory had some elegance about it. Elegant theories are no substitute for hard cash at the supermarket checkout.

Realistic share investing

Successful share investing calls for something more realistic than deciding on asset allocation figures and investing the appropriate amount in stocks without regard to market cycles and the consequent amount of market risk.

What is needed is a two stage process. First, make policy decisions, based on the situation of each investor, as to the minimum and maximum percentages of total capital to go into shares (and other investments). That is the semi-permanent policy range.

The second stage is to make medium term timing decisions. This involves considering current level of stock prices against objective standards to decide whether the amount invested in shares should be increased towards the upper limit of the policy range, or reduced towards the lower limit or somewhere in between.

◆ *Medium term timing is practicable*

Though attempts to make short term timing decisions are generally futile, it is a different matter with medium term timing. Stock markets in the medium to long term tend to regress to the mean. So a study of long term market behaviour can reveal when the market is at levels so far above normal — in terms of indicators such as average dividend yield or long term price trend. In those circumstances a decline back towards the mean is highly likely and further sustained gain unlikely (or vice versa when it is well below normal).

◆ *Ranking the market by zones*

So it is possible to rank the position of the market in zones ranging from 5 — for very favourable, i.e good prospects of sustained gain with limited downside risk — to 1 (most unfavourable with limited prospects of sustained gain and relatively high downside risk). Sensible and gradual increase in stock investment as the market moves towards Zone 5 and reduction as it moves towards Zone 1 can produce superior results.

◆ *Definition of zones*

Based on experience of the last 35 years, the market can be divided into five zones for various ranges of price dividend multiples or dividend yields. Zone 5 is the range of the lowest price dividend multiples, i.e the highest average dividend yield and Zone 1 is the reverse. (See table overleaf.)

Zone	Average Dividend Yield
5	5.50% and above
4	4.60% to 5.49%
3	4.10% to 4.59%
2	3.70% to 4.09%
1	2.20% to 3.69%

What the record shows

Set out below are five-year capital gain figures for investing in different zones. Remember, Zone 5 covers the *lowest* price dividend multiple, i.e. the *highest* average dividend yields. Zone 1 covers the highest price dividend multiples, i.e. the lowest average dividend yield. The figures are for capital gain per cent per annum over five year periods:

Zone	Average (%)	Minimum (%)	Co-eff. of Variation
5	14.9	1.7	0.49
4	7.3	-6.58	0.95
3	4.9	-10.0	1.34
2	4.0	-15.3	2.1
1	0.6	-14.2	9.6

By comparing the Zone 5 figures with the Zone 1 figures, the vast difference between investing in Zone 5 and Zone 1 can be seen.

Average — The average gain of 14.9 per cent in Zone 5 is 24 times as high as the average of 0.6 per cent in Zone 1.

Downside — In Zone 5, the worst result was a small gain of 1.7 per cent compared with a large loss of 14.2 per cent in Zone 1. As those are annual rates, they represent a gain of 9 per cent and a loss of 54 per cent over five years, respectfully.

Variability — The last column, the co-efficient of variation (standard deviation dividend by the mean) is a means of comparing the degree of variability. In this context a co-efficient of variation can be seen as an indication of stability in gains or losses, with lower co-efficient of variation indicating stability. So Zone 5 with a co-efficient of 0.49 is almost 20 times as stable as Zone 1 with a co-efficient of 9.6.

Other measures — The above figures are related to capital gain. But figures for total return, including income and capital that are discussed in later chapters, show a similar pattern. So does a comparison of total return on shares compared with the return on five year Treasury Bonds.

Similar experience overseas — My research into the British and US markets shows a similar pattern. The eminent US investment specialist, John Bogle, in his book *Bogle on Mutual Funds*, put it this way (p. 250):

> *"Even more simplistically, but offered without apology, the stock market can be viewed as a game of chance: the odds change along with changes in the yields prevailing at the time of your investment. During the 1926-92 period, the stock market provided a total return averaging about +10% annually. The chance of reaching or exceeding this average during any ten year period has been shaped importantly by the initial dividend yield at the start of each period, as shown in Table 12-5"*

The table referred to by John Bogle shows that the chance of a return greater than 10 per cent over subsequent decades from investing at various dividend yields was:

Initial Yield	Chance of Achieving
Less than 3.5%	1 in 16
3.5% to 4.5%	7 in 15
4.6% to 6.0%	13 in 17
More than 6%	6 in 10

Expressed as percentages, the achievement figures are 6 per cent, 47 per cent, 76 per cent and 60 per cent. The last two figures are 13 and 10 times the success rate for investing on a low dividend yield of less than 3.5 per cent, i.e. a price dividend multiple of more than 28.6.

Summary — So it is manifestly clear, on the basis of past experience, that a strategy of increasing share market investment in Zones 5 or 4 and reducing it in Zones 2 or 1 will produce considerably better results than following the widely promoted fallacy that timing does not matter.

The above elements are the core of the most practical approach to stock investing which has emerged during my 40 years in the investment business. Coupled with more realistic analysis of company earnings and other matters, it is the basis of investment practice outlined in this book. It is based on the testing of all of the approaches discussed above and other investment theories in the course of my work, including research associated with writing many books on the subject and over 200 issues of an investment newsletter.

The suggested approach is not put forward as a sure way to riches. Far from it. I constantly advise investors to avoid any investment theory or practice which is promoted as the one infallible way to make a lot of money. However, experience shows clearly that the practices described in this book increase the possibility of making good profits and minimise the chance of making severe losses.

The latter is an important point. There is an old Scotch proverb that any fool can make money but it takes a wise person to save it. In the investment world, many investors make good profits in a boom. The trick is to ensure that the profits made in a boom are not severely eroded in the almost inevitable slump that follows.

The elements of sound share market investment practice involve the following:

> **Knowledge** — You need to know the components of total return and their significance, the nature of the stock market, namely that it is volatile and unstable, the

dimensions of the stock market (as discussed at the end of this chapter), the importance of timing and realistic analysis.

➣ **Psychology and traps in popular theories** — There are serious weaknesses in popular theories such as the efficient market hypothesis and the capital asset pricing model — mainly because they fail to take into account the influence on the stock market of the risk concealers, mob psychology, the herd instinct, and changes in investing fads and the flavour of the year stocks or industries.

➣ **Recognition of risk, policy and strategy** — Recognise the reality of risk including market and information risk and beware of the risk concealers. Investors should develop a policy that recognises each investor's ability to face risk and a strategy for putting that policy into effect in the light of changing market trends.

➣ **Operational decisions** — Develop a capacity to take selling decisions, concentrate on less well known stocks, review portfolios on the basis of current values, position and prospects, operate a portfolio which is well spread but compact, use realistic rather than conventional analysis of trends in the economy and corporate sector and in company earnings, and remember the vast difference between the reality and rhetoric in managed funds.

Those elements are discussed in later chapters and condensed into a set of principles in Chapter Twenty-two.

The dimensions of the stock market

An explorer or traveller would not go into a new area without studying a map to see the heights of peaks and the depths of valleys. But many people making share investments are encouraged to do so without being given a clear idea of the peaks and troughs, or the time the market may stay in the valley until it recovers and scales new heights.

Worse than that, they are often given a picture that is false. This may be due to deliberate action by fund managers or commission-driven advisers gilding the lily to earn more profits. Or the misleading impression may be gained from discussions with people of goodwill whose failing is that they pass on the common platitudes of the conventional investment wisdom which are often incorrect. Uncritical acceptance of well established fallacies and passing them on to clients may have caused just as serious losses to investors as deliberately misleading information. To put it another way, share investors are often the victims of the process which is explained earlier, called "Goebbeling".

The map or dimensions of the share market which all stock investors need to be given would include the following highlights:

➤ **Average long term results** — If investors' experience happened to be average the total return from income and capital movement would be about 11.7 per cent per annum. Generally, that would be better than other investments.

➤ **Components of results** — The results of stock market investments comprise four components, namely initial dividend yield, a gradual increase in dividend income, the dividend tax credit on some shares and increase or decrease in share prices. Generally, the change in share prices is the most significant component of overall profit or loss on share investments. Moreover, the trend in the market as a whole is often the most significant factor in the movement in individual stock returns.

➤ **Retained earnings not a component** — Contrary to popular impressions, retained earnings, i.e. the portion of earnings which is not paid as dividends are not a component of return on share investments. Those earnings and later profits generated by them may tend to increase share prices, but it does not always work out that way. Cyclical movements, reaction to earlier excesses or changes in the mood of the market have often prevented the expected price rise from that source.

➤ **Wide variation** — As the results for many investors may differ greatly from the average, it is important to be aware of the extent of the variations especially in the most volatile factor, namely price movements.

> **Periods of no joy** — There have been periods of up to 15 years for the All Ordinaries Index (from 1959 to 1974) and 23 years for the All Mining Index (from December 1969 to February 1993) in which there has been no sustained net gain.

The above dimensions of the share market should be remembered as the framework within which all of the material in subsequent chapters is to be considered.

Shares compared with other investments

As indicated already, in the long term, shares generally provide better results than other investments. But like property or any market-based investment, the results can vary greatly depending on timing and to a lesser extent analysis of economic trends and company prospects.

Compared with real estate investments, shares are similar in one respect. It is that both are medium risk investments which generally offer better long term returns, including capital gain, than fixed-interest investments, but with the risk of market fluctuation referred to above.

One advantage of shares over real estate is their liquidity. Generally, they can be turned into cash readily, except for some periods of extreme market weakness when listed stocks in medium to smaller companies may not be so saleable.

Another significant advantage is that selling and buying decisions do not have to be on an all-or-nothing basis as for owners of property. Share investors can use the step system of buying and selling gradually.

Generally, the information available in relation to share prices is far more reliable than that available to investors in property. There is not as much reliable information about the rate of change in real estate values as there is for share values. Widely publicised claims about a more or less steady upward rise in real estate values and high rates of capital growth are not accurate.

One relative disadvantage of shares is that share investors do not have anything like the same degree of control over their investments as investors in property. Property investors can make their own decisions on whether to extend or improve their properties, or to increase or reduce rentals. But in share investments, except for very large investors, there is no real control over the actions of the board of directors and management of the company in which they hold shares.

Shareholder discounts

Another attraction of shares is that some companies offer discounts on purchases by shareholders, generally subject to a minimum holding of about $2000 worth of shares. One such company is Coles Myer Ltd, with discounts of 5 per cent to 10 per cent on purchases by shareholders at all of the stores in that group, including Coles supermarkets, Myer department stores, K Mart, Target, OfficeWorks Superstores and others.

An article in the December 1994 issue of *Donnelly's Investing Today* points out that the discount could increase the after-tax income return on Coles Myer stores to more than double the return on Woolworths shares. Details of companies offering shareholder discounts can be obtained from brokers or company offices.

The fact that a company offers discounts is, of course, not the only factor to consider in making investment decisions.

Chapter 2

Market Lessons
from the Last
10 to 40 Years

Much market comment is not factual

Probably the most important single lesson that I have learned
as the result of 40 years investment experience could be
summarised as under:

> *"Never in the whole history of investing have so many
> people made so many statements with so few facts to
> support them".*

That paraphrase of Winston Churchill's famous tribute to the
fighter pilots of the Royal Air Force in the Battle of Britain in
1940 is a good summary of the situation in relation to stock
markets in the Australia and other parts of the world.

Matters to consider

Only by looking back at market performance over the last 10
to 40 years is it possible to fully understand the reality of the
long term trend in stock markets.

Investors need to make wise decisions based on realities
rather than the inaccurate picture often portrayed by the
conventional wisdom. In particular, it is necessary to be aware
of the following matters.

◆ *Non recurring factors*

Before accepting performance figures for very long periods
from 20 to 100 years, consider how those figures may have
been significantly affected by non recurring forces which may
be absent or less significant in the future.

◆ *The fallacy of aggregation*

The likelihood of gaining a false impression of possible future
trends on the basis of figures for very long periods. Good

performance for a long period of 50 years may be the net result of two different forces:

➤ Extremely good results for the first part of the period

➤ Relatively disappointing results for the later portion.

For example, a reasonably good result of 8 per cent per annum compound over 50 years could reflect an excellent result of 12 per cent per annum compound for the first 25 years and a poor result of 4 per cent per annum compound for the second 25 years. As the results for the later half of the 50 year period may be more like what could be expected in the future, those who are persuaded to invest on the basis of the 50 year performance of 8 per cent per annum may be very disappointed if future results are closer to 4 per cent per annum compound.

◆ *Changed investing conditions*

Analysis may show that a significant factor in the very good long term results achieved over 20 or 30 years or more, was that the investment was made on an initial dividend yield of 5 per cent per annum or more. That good income figure plus gradual increase in dividend income would mean that even modest capital gain would produce a good overall return of 14 per cent or more. It would not be realistic to expect anything like the same sort of result from investing at the market peak, in February 1994, when the initial dividend yield was about 2.8 per cent.

To produce the same overall performance for those who invest when the average dividend yield is 2.8 per cent, a much greater amount of capital gain would be required. But a moment's thought would show that this low dividend yield was the result of share prices being pushed up to relatively high levels. So in the medium term the market is more likely to produce less than average capital gain or even capital loss rather than the required amount of above average gain. It is a case of a greater need for capital gain and a diminished capacity to produce that gain.

◆ *Good times do not last — Abraham Lincoln's comment*

According to a statement attributed to Abraham Lincoln about 150 years ago, you can fool all of the people some of the time, or some of the people all of the time, but you cannot fool all of the people all of the time. For ordinary shares this could be paraphrased to say that the market can produce high rates of increase for some of the time, or medium rates of increases all of the time, but it cannot produce high rates of increase all of the time.

The stock market 40 years ago and now

The stock market 40 years ago when I moved into the investment business was vastly different from the market today. Consideration of a few of those differences should be sufficient to show that:

➢ It may not be wise to buy shares or unit trusts just because of very long term performance figures

➢ Decisions to invest need to be made after assessing whether stocks are highly priced, reasonably priced or low priced on objective criteria such as average dividend yield and long term trends.

◆ *Dividend yield and interest rates*

In the early fifties, the market average dividend yield was not only high in absolute figures but high related to the cost of money and interest rates. For example, in January 1951 the average dividend yield of 6.34 per cent was more than twice the medium term interest rate of about 3 per cent. In those days, investors demanded a higher income return on shares because of the higher risk. With this flying start, if capital gain averaged as little as about 2.7 per cent per annum the total return on shares would be three times the fixed-interest return.

That was a long way from the situation in more recent years. Near the peak of the boom in 1987 the average dividend yield was about 2.2 per cent compared with medium term fixed-interest rate of about 12 per cent. These figures can be seen in better perspective in the table overleaf by expressing them in terms of relative cost which is interest rate divided by dividend yield.

Time	Dividend Yield (%)	Interest Rate (%)	Relative Cost
January 1951	6.34	3	0.47
August 1987	2.2	12	5.5

Let us now look at the time when share prices were at their lowest in the 1980s and hence average dividend yield was at its highest, namely August 1982. The average dividend yield was 6.32 per cent and the medium term interest rate about 12.5 per cent. So the relative cost figure was 1.98 — far from the bargain basement figures of 0.43 in the 1950s.

◆ *Other differences*

Forty years ago superannuation funds and financial institutions were not nearly as significant players in the share market as they have been in the last 25 years or so. Individual interest in the stock market both directly and indirectly through mutual funds was negligible by comparison with the present situation. There was nothing like the present very great promotion of and interest in shares in the media, in academia, and in the broader community.

Effect of non recurring factors

It is sometimes argued that the wider public interest in the stock market — the large number of people including stock brokers, financial planners, fund managers and life insurance companies — provide a solid foundation and buying support for the market. This is true up to a point. But in considering the impact of those forces on the market you need to recognise that it is highly unlikely that in the next 10, 20, 30, or 40 years the buying support from those sources will increase at anything like the rate at which it has increased during the last 40 years.

◆ *Acceptance of lower dividend yields*

Over the last 40 years there has been a definite trend towards lower dividend yields. Naturally, dividend yields have varied inversely with share prices. But there has been a trend towards lower dividend yield which is clearly shown in the relative cost figures above. The prevailing view 40 years ago that the income returns from common stocks should be higher than the current medium term interest rates to allow for the greater risk, has been replaced by a view that dividends are of little account. The conventional wisdom seems to believe that because common stocks will produce good capital gain, little if any attention should be given to dividend yield.

The point has been made in Chapter One that a good deal of investment thought and practice implies that it is earnings that count and that undistributed earnings will be reflected in increased share prices. But the reality is different.

◆ *Can the trend continue?*

It is highly unlikely that the long term trend towards lower dividend yields can continue at anything like the rate of the last 40 years. At the peak of the market, in January 1994, the gap between average dividend yields and management charges of unit trusts was very small. In some trusts, the annual management charges were absorbing about three quarters of income.

If stock prices had continued to rise as fast as many enthusiastic comments had suggested, then before too long the management charges would exceed the dividend income. Computers in fund managers' offices would need to be reprogrammed to send with income statements a debit note for the deficit rather than the traditional cheque.

So the impetus to rising stock prices from this source may continue but probably be much less significant than in the past.

◆ *The efficient market hypothesis*

For decades, thousands of finance executives were educated by academics in some institutions which were devoted to this theory with all the zeal of the old-fashioned religious fanatic. It certainly helped fund managers and financial planners to promote the incorrect notion that it is always a good time to buy shares. It tended to give an air of academic virtue to apathetic fund managers who failed to take protective action when there were signs that a cyclical slump could be imminent.

So it was probably a very significant factor in supporting share prices. Now that it is being seriously challenged and severely criticised (see the comments in Chapter One), there will probably be fewer people prepared to think that the whole stock market or an individual stock is good buying at whatever the current price may be.

Summary of changed conditions

With each of the above favourable factors likely to be considerably less significant in the future than over the past 40 years it would be unwise to make investment decisions solely on some aspects of the conventional wisdom. Instead, it is desirable to concentrate buying at times when stocks are more reasonably priced on the basis of dividend yields, namely when they are in Zones 4 or 5. The figures in Chapter One show how investment at those times has generally produced far better results with much lower downside risk than investing at other times.

Beware of misleading claims

In recent years, many investment decisions have been made on the basis of information that is misleading or is a dangerous half truth. The problem is that many fund managers, who claim that timing does not matter, must in fact believe that it does. In promoting the benefits of share market investments, they generally support their claims with performance figures carefully selected to reflect the periods in which the market did very well, i.e. the periods which are far from typical.

A classic case was a series of advertisements which highlighted the gain of over 300 per cent in capital value of a trust over the previous 15 years. What the advertisement failed to state was that after very high gains over the first 10 years, the value had declined significantly over the last five years. It also failed to point out that, overall, the previous 15 years had been by far the best 15 years this century and it was highly unlikely that those well above average results would be repeated.

Investors must remember these points:

➤ The real dimensions of the share market are described in Chapter One, including the wide variation in capital value, the fact that recovery from a slump has taken up to 10 years, and that there have been periods of 15 years in which the All Ordinaries Index has shown no sustained net gain.

➤ The figures in Chapter One and the reference to the figures on the US market show clearly that the initial average dividend yield has a great influence on investment results. That means that the periods when a boom has pushed share prices up and yields down — when share investments are very popular and pressure to buy shares or equity trusts is extreme — are the periods in which it is wise to decrease rather than increase share investing.

The future and regression to the mean

One of the points made by John Bogle in his book which is referred to in Chapter One, is that there is a tendency for stock markets and other financial data to regress to the mean. After periods of above average or below average performance, there is often a reaction to bring the long term performance closer to the average. From the above figures, it is apparent that the market has shown an ability to continue producing above average results for fairly long periods of up to 15 years before the reaction sets in.

Chapter 3

The Need to
Recognise all
Kinds of Risk

Return *of* capital or return *on* capital

"I am not concerned about a return *on* my capital; all I am worried about is the return *of* my capital". That comment, made during the depression by comedian Eddie Cantor, is a reminder that the safety of capital and the degree of risk to which it is exposed is a vital factor for investors.

Risk, as far as many investment people and authors of investment books are concerned, is the original four letter word which is never mentioned. You can look through the index of some well known investment books and find few, if any, references to risk. In reports of investment advisers making glowing recommendations of various investments, risk is often conspicuous by its absence.

Recognising risk to achieve wealth that stays

According to the old Scottish proverb, which I quoted in Chapter One, any fool can make money but it takes a wise man to save it. In investing in stock markets, and indeed in other investments, it could be said that achieving wealth is not the hard part. The hard part is achieving wealth that stays rather than wealth that disappears when a boom turns into a slump.

Essentially this comes down to recognising risk. In recent years, the best results have been achieved by those people who recognised, prior to major slumps, that the frantic rise of the previous months or years could not be maintained. Because they knew there was a significant risk of capital gains being eroded by a more or less inevitable slump, they sold at least part of their share holdings. As well as converting the "maybe money" of "paper profits" into the "actual money "of realised gains, this action protected their capital from the erosion that would have followed in the slump.

It is important to be ever aware of risks and to realise that there are many different types of risks. Some types of risk, for example, the risk that if a company goes broke you will lose all your money in that stock, are widely recognised. But a number of other risks are not so well known.

Financial risk

What many investors do not realise is that an important matter for them to consider is the question of financial risk. In deciding whether to buy stocks, or to continue to hold shares in your portfolio, you have to consider whether those stocks are exposed to significant financial risk. The companies that are exposed to that risk are those which have borrowed heavily to expand rapidly or to take advantages of favourable conditions.

So long as conditions remain favourable, the companies that have borrowed heavily or worked on an unsound and unbalanced financial structure, may get by. But when troubles come in the form of difficult trading conditions in a recession, or rising interest rates, or both, they may face severe financial problems and the risk of total failure.

For investors, there is a financial risk associated with borrowing to increase their returns, whether on share investments or on other types of investments. Through the multiplying effect, gearing can increase results significantly when things are going well. But in difficult conditions, such as a market slump, the multiplying effect works the other way.

For example, when the gearing ratio is 4, i.e. total investment equals four times the amount of investors' capital with the balance being borrowed, a decline in value of 40 per cent on the stocks can mean a loss of 160 per cent of the investors' capital — plus the net after tax cost of interest.

Market risk

Probably the most significant risk faced by investors in shares is the risk which is seldom discussed, namely market risk. That is the risk that significant losses can occur, even in shares of very sound companies with good records and prospects, simply as the result of market fluctuation.

A point that many investors often overlook is that slumps are no respecters of prestigious names. The so called leaders and the most prestigious stocks tend to get swept along with the downward tide. No matter how well managed a company may be, no matter how good its future prospects, no matter how sound its financial position or how impressive its earnings record has been, it is not immune to the law of gravity. The old saying that what goes up must come down is as true of stocks, including market leaders, as of other areas.

How the mighty have fallen

Set out below is an extract from my book *The Three Rs of Investing — Return Risk and Relativity*, (p.63, George Allen & Unwin Australia Pty Ltd, Sydney 1985). The point that well-known and highly regarded stocks are not immune to the law of gravity can be seen from the following list showing percentage declines in some well-known stocks in the years between 1968 and 1974.

Stock	Percentage of Decline
BHP	78
Lend Lease	78
MIM	77
TNT	77
Brambles Industry	76
Consolidated Press	74
Bank of New South Wales (Now Westpac)	68

It would be fair to say that the vast bulk of the significant decline in all these stocks was due to market factor, generally reaction to excessive enthusiasm of an earlier period. It was not due to any collapse in earnings, as many of the stocks maintained their earnings fairly well over the period and others experienced relatively small declines in earnings compared to the declines in share values

♦   *BHP — a very risky stock*

The importance of market fluctuations on the risk of even the most prestigious stocks can be seen from a study of BHP share prices. After the massive gain in August 1968 it has performed as follows:

➤ A net decline of 78 per cent or about 20 per cent per annum in the next six years to September 1974.

➤ A net increase of about 8 per cent per annum over the next nine years to 1983.

➤ A net gain of about 12.7 per cent in the period of just under 12 years to February 1995.

➤ For the 26.5 years from August 1968 to February 1995 a net gain of 7.3 per cent per annum.

Accounting and information risk

Another risk that has to be considered is the accounting or information risk. Many investors in the last few years suffered substantial losses because they bought shares in companies, or continued to hold them, on the basis of unreliable information in the published financial statements.

Unfortunately, they thought that they could rely on financial statements which some leading firms of auditors had reported as being true and fair. For a number of reasons the sad fact is that investors just cannot consider that audited financial statements contain reliable information.

One is the fact that directors who wish to portray an inadequate or misleading picture can generally do so by a process of convoluted transactions in which the form of the transaction appears to comply with accounting standards. But the substance of the transaction is completely different — for example, by recording profits on sales where put options enable the buyer to, in effect, reverse the sale at his discretion so that in reality a real sale has not been made.

Apart from the accounting risk, there is a risk as to reliability of other information. Sometimes information issued by companies to Stock Exchanges may be inadequate, or can be examples of dangerous half-truths to which reference has already been made in another context.

For those who invest in shares indirectly through unit trusts, information in the prospectuses is sometimes inaccurate, inadequate or misleading. It tends to convey the common view of the market as moving steadily upward with any decline being a temporary mental aberration from which the market will soon recover to return to its preordained steadily upward trend.

The picture portrayed in most mutual fund prospectuses tends to ignore some of the realities discussed in Chapter One such as the these:

➢ **Timing** — The vast difference in results achieved from investing near the peak of the cycle just before a slump commences, compared with investing at or near a low point before a bull market commences.

➢ **Wide variation** — The fact that capital gain, even over a period as long as five years, has varied from a massive gain of over 330 per cent to a loss of 57 per cent of capital.

➢ **Periods of no joy** — There have been periods of up to 15 years for the All Ordinaries Index and 23 years for the All Mining Index in which there have been no sustained net gain.

Major risk not covered by spread

Good investment practice, and indeed common sense, suggests it is wise to have funds spread over a number of different investments, rather than having all your eggs in one or a couple of baskets. This procedure is a step in the right direction. But it provides protection only against one type of risk, namely specific risk, i.e. the risk of failure of one particular company.

It is no protection against the other, and generally more significant type of risk, namely market risk, or what is called systemic risk. In any general share market decline, even if you have a portfolio which is well spread over a number of companies, you will see a significant amount of your capital eroded.

The common myth that you will always be in good shape if you spread your funds roughly equally over shares, property, and fixed-interest investments or cash, is misleading because it overlooks the importance of market factors. For example, people who had their portfolios constructed in that way would have seen at various times in the past a decline, of up to 40 per cent or 50 per cent, in both the share and property component of their portfolios. That would have had a far more serious effect on their overall capital than they would have expected from the bland comments that a spread of that type is a good way of keeping the capital safe.

Risk of relying on alleged expertise of managers

Many investors have lost a lot of money in the last few years because they were not aware of the risk of relying on the alleged expertise of managers of equity trusts. They were told, very often by financial planners or brokers or fund sales people, that the expertise of managers in some way made their investments more secure. The truth is that the underlying investments can be affected by cyclical slumps. Moreover, records show that, except for a small minority, managers fail to do any better than the market average.

How speculative are "blue chips"?

The conventional investment wisdom treats as speculative investments, only those involved in high risk business, such as mineral exploration stocks or some new ventures. But the reality is different.

When you consider the realities of market cycles and the list of losses given in the table earlier of over 70 per cent in highly regarded stocks, it is not logical to suggest that well established stocks are not to some extent speculative.

The situation is that in any market investment, such as shares or property, there is inevitably a great deal of speculation. When people buy shares, they are speculating that because of prospects of increased dividends, or some other cause, the market at a later stage will be prepared to pay a higher price for those shares and thus give them a profit.

In effect, there is a form of fairly sophisticated, fairly intensive and fairly large scale speculation by investment institutions as they try to out-guess each other as to which shares will perform better, or whether over a period the stock market will perform better than other investments.

Shares in good companies may be speculative

To say that shares, even in the best known and highly regarded companies, are to some extent speculative investments, is not by any means a criticism of those companies or the people involved in their management. It is simply a recognition of the reality that the share prices are affected by fluctuations in the market in which speculation can sometimes have a very significant influence.

Changes in market sentiment, or to put it another way, in the speculative interest in various stocks, can often, for some periods have a more significant effect on the results to investors than the earnings and prospects of the company.

About 60 years ago, the late Lord Keynes, wrote in his famous book, *The General Theory*:

"Speculation does no harm as bubbles on a steady stream of enterprise, but the position is serious when enterprise becomes a bubble on a whirlpool of speculation. When the job of raising capital in a country becomes the by-product of the activities of a casino, the task is not likely to be well done".

Those who have studied movements in share and other markets over the last ten years or so, would have to agree that nothing much has changed in the last 60 years.

Currency risk in international stocks

Investors in international shares or in unit trusts which invest in international shares have to face currency risk as well as market risk. If the international stock market in which they invest declines by 40 per cent, and during the relevant period the value of the international currency declines relative to the Australian currency by 30 per cent, there is a very large combined loss.

34

At other times there may be a dual gain from favourable movements in both the international market and in currency movements. Sometimes a favourable movement in the international market may partly, or completely, offset an unfavourable currency movement.

If international investments are spread over stocks in several different currencies, there may be some protection from the spread of currency risk with unfavourable movements in one currency being offset by favourable movements in another.

At least that is the theory, but protection through spread over different currencies may not always work. There have been times when the value of several major international currencies has moved in the same direction relative to the Australian currency. So a spread may be ineffective or only partly effective in minimising currency risk.

Some protection against currency risk may be obtained by hedging techniques either by the individual investor or the unit trust manager.

An investor considering investing internationally should recognise the reality of currency risk and study the availability and cost of any hedging protection.

Accepting reasonable risk in seeking higher returns

It is still true to say that nothing attempted, nothing gained. To achieve better results from investments than can be achieved in the very safe low risk investments, some degree of risk must be taken. But, it is important that in deciding what policy to be followed, (a matter discussed in Chapter Six), investors are fully aware of the various types of risks, especially market risk in deciding what portion of their capital should be exposed to that type of risk.

Chapter 4

The Vast Difference
Between Reality
and Widespread
Fallacies

*"It can be mighty cold in Melbourne
in winter without a shirt"*

That was the title of an article I wrote some years ago. It referred to a comment made by a Melbourne investment specialist, some years ago, to the effect that resource stocks would be so good in the seventies that you could put your shirt on them. It pointed out that if he had followed his own advice and put his shirt on those stocks, he would have been without his shirt through 18 of the next 23 winters.

During the next two decades there were some temporary recoveries from the peak of that market early in 1970 when the statement was made. But until 1993 they were not sustained. In the early months of 1993, would you believe, the index for the stocks on which the specialist said you should put your shirt, was lower than it was 23 years ago.

This is a good illustration of how dangerous it is to accept so many statements which are made about investments. Financial fables, fallacies and folklore abound in relation to investment in stocks and it is important that investors be aware of them.

Invalid theories

In the discussion in Chapter One on the development of investment theory and practice, there was a reference to weaknesses in some investment theories which had been popular over the last 40 years, including the capital asset pricing model and the efficient market hypothesis. Strong

36

criticisms of the latter concept by Professor R. Shiller and George Soros were quoted.

Set out below is a summary of the differences between reality and popular theories including those two concepts:

♦ *Decision making*

The theory — Investors act rationally in making investment decisions

The reality — Decisions are made by human beings with likes, dislikes prejudices and other human qualities. Many of the decisions are made by people who fall in love with particular stocks.

In any case, even if investors were perfectly rational, the information presented to them is distorted by investment people either deliberately to make more money or unwittingly by uncritically accepting market platitudes. So even if investors were capable of acting rationally at all times, the decisions in many cases would not be rational, because they would be based on false information. The result would be a case, as data processing people say, of garbage in, garbage out.

♦ *Investors are risk averse*

The theory — Investors are averse to risk, so they would require a higher return on investments on which the risk is higher.

The reality — Investors may try to be risk averse and may think that they are risk averse but in many cases they are not and cannot be risk averse. The reason is that to be averse to risk you must be aware of the risk. Young children or people from primitive cultures would touch a live electric wire because they are not aware of the risk of doing so.

Investors are not aware of a great deal of the risk involved in various types of investments because the people on whom they rely for information are in the very profitable investment business activity of risk concealing — for example, by not informing investors of the wide range of results of share investing, of the great difference in results achieved by investing when stocks are reasonably priced compared with investing near the top of a boom just before a major slump.

◆ *Information is readily available*

The theory — Relevant information, especially about shares is widely publicised and readily available.

The reality — Though there is much objective information available, it is swamped by other material which is a good deal less than objective. This includes accounting anomalies, interpretation of information by analysts in broking offices, unit trust company executives with stock options, self-servicing comments by managers and commission-based financial planners who have a significant financial interest in presenting information which will encourage purchase of equity trusts.

◆ *Stock markets are efficient*

The theory — Because information is readily available, the price of a particular stock or the overall position of a market at any time reflects the best unbiased estimate of what they should be. Hence, nothing is to be gained by selecting stocks or endeavouring to time moves into or out of the market. In the long term, no investing strategy will produce better results, after allowing for transaction costs and risk, than the passive strategy of buying and holding.

The reality — The decline of 20 per cent in stock prices in one day in the October 1987 market crash cannot be explained away by any new information that emerged on that day. Nor can other anomalies such as well documented month and week day effects, or periodical excessive enthusiasm in buying panics that have occurred for example in conglomerates, high tech stocks and other segments with which the market becomes obsessed from time to time.

Some mutual funds and professional investors such as Warren Buffett of Berkshire Hathaway and George Soros have demonstrated an ability to consistently outperform the market in the long term. In the papers in the book *Advances in Behavioural Finance* which is quoted in Chapter One, there are studies on the effect on the stock market of fads and psychological factors which the efficient market hypothesis fails to consider. As George Soros has pointed out in the quote in Chapter One, the more people who believe in the efficient market the more unstable the market will be.

♦ *Volatility is a measure of risk*

The theory — Volatility measured by the standard deviation is a measure of the risk of the market.

The reality — As risk is defined as the chance of a bad result, what investors need as a measure of risk is an indication of what, on the basis of past experience, is the worst capital loss that could be suffered. For the stock market, even over a five year period that figure is a loss of 57 per cent. A false impression of risk can be created by the use of volatility figures as the calculations give similar weight to upward as to downward movements.

Moreover the use of volatility to measure risk, produces the absurd proposition that on the day after the 1987 crash the market was more risky than the day before. But it is obvious that after a decline to a lower level the risk must have reduced not increased.

♦ *Beta figures*

The theory — Beta figures indicate how a particular stock reacts to a rise or fall in the overall market. A stock with a beta of 2 would rise or fall twice as much as the overall market with a beta of 1, at the same rate as the overall market and with a beta of 0.5 half as much as the overall market.

The reality — There is considerable doubt as to whether betas are stationary over time. If they are not, then, betas calculated on the basis of past figures may not be relevant in the future. In any case, the betas are based on overall market movement and the overall market is generally a medium risk area, so a stock with a beta of 1 or less may still involve some considerable risk. At times when a boom has pushed prices up to unrealistic levels and experience suggests that a slump is more or less inevitable, the whole market then becomes a high risk investment area. Hence, even if betas were stationary over time, the base against which they are measured is unstable.

♦ *Economic trends and market changes*

The theory — Thorough economic analysis will produce good results for the investor in shares because the share market reflects economic trends.

The reality — The share market has a life of its own which for considerable periods may move faster or slower than economic trends and at times in the opposite direction. The difference is due partly to a tendency for the share market to over-anticipate favourable developments. Then, when the inevitable reaction sets in, the market may decline sharply with share prices falling despite a rising trend in dividends per share and earnings per share.

The classic example of this reality is that the share market has gone for long periods of up to 15 years without any sustained net gain — despite generally favourable results for the economy and corporate earnings.

That is why some very successful investors remember two old adages — namely, "anticipation is greater than realisation" and that "it can pay to buy on rumour and sell on fact".

It also is a reminder that it may be unwise to buy shares solely on the basis of expected improvement in economic conditions, corporate profits, or favourable factors for the industry and company. A study of the market may show that, as a result of a recent boom, those favourable factors have already been anticipated and perhaps over-anticipated by the market.

♦ *The random walk*

The theory — Share market prices reflect reaction to a wide range of information which comes to the market in a random fashion. So they are no more predictable than the wanderings of an intoxicated person.

The reality — The random walk theory is probably valid in the short term (which is the area in which all or most of the studies to support the theory have been conducted) but not in the longer term.

Studies show that in the long term stock markets, like other markets, tend to have a normal trading range in bands above and below their long term trend in which all trading activity occurs for about two thirds of the time. When prices are in the upper phase of the more or less cyclical pattern, the medium term results from investing at that time tend to be disappointing and downside risk greater than when prices are below or not far above the long term trend. Another indicator of whether the market may be approaching dangerously high levels is the average dividend yield. (See comments in Chapter One on Zones 1 to 5.)

♦ *Timing does not matter*

The theory — Because of the random walk theory and the efficient market hypothesis, nothing is to be gained from trying to time moves into or out of the market.

The reality — Though attempts to pick short term turning points are generally futile, medium term timing, using the Zones referred to in Chapter One, is a practicable approach. The record clearly shows that there is a vast difference between investing in Zone 5 and Zone 1. Even moderate success in increasing share market investment, as the market moves towards Zones 4 and 5, and reducing it as it moves towards Zones 2 and 1 can improve investment returns greatly — with results considerably better than following the conventional wisdom of the jelly fish philosophy of just drifting up and down with the market tide.

Misleading labels

♦ *"Growth stocks"*

Many investors have suffered serious losses in recent years because there is no truth in labelling laws in relation to share market investments, and indeed, investments generally. For example, the term "growth stock" and "growth trust" are still widely used despite the fact that many of these stocks and trusts have gone through very long periods when they have failed to produce growth, and instead have caused substantial losses. (See the list in Chapter Three of large declines by highly regarded stocks.)

◆ *"Blue Chips"*

This term, together with similar phrases such as leading stocks, or quality stocks, is also misleading. The term implies that they would give the investor some safe haven against extreme fluctuations. The reality is that stocks to which those prestigious terms are applied, often provide no protection against the effect of market declines.

Pointing out these facts does not mean that you should never invest in those stocks. For some investors, and at some times, they produce very good results, and no doubt will continue to do so in the future. But the important point is to be on your guard against the unsound decisions which can be made by relying on these labels which are often misleading.

The inflation hedge fallacy

A very popular fallacy is that shares, and indeed a number of other investments, provide a hedge against inflation. The reality is that there is no investment that can properly be described as an inflation hedge. To be an inflation hedge, the investment would need to provide adequate and sustained gain from a purchase at any time and at any price.

The reality is that, at times, stocks can produce capital gain which is more than adequate to offset inflation. But at other times, share prices may lag well behind inflation.

The inability of any investment to be properly described as an inflation hedge was summed up about 150 years ago by Abraham Lincoln. The statement attributed to him which has been quoted previously is that you can fool all of the people some of the time, or some of the people all of the time, but you cannot fool all of the people all of the time.

So when a boom has pushed prices higher and ever higher, it only remains for some of the investors to become unfooled about the hype of the moment. By ceasing to buy and perhaps selling to take a profit, they will probably cause prices at first to falter, and then as further people become unfooled, a slump can get under way.

The bigger fool theory

Talking of fools, another theory is the bigger fool theory. This theory states that in a boom in the share market or elsewhere, it is often profitable to buy at a foolish price, because before too long an even bigger fool will come along, and pay an even more foolish price. This theory is fine, but there is a problem. (There is always a problem with fine theories.) The problem is that the supply of fools is not limitless. So, the important thing is to ensure that you are no later than the second last fool when the crunch comes, and the boom is turned into a slump.

Fallacies about share market performance

The figures in earlier chapters showed the difference between the reality of share price movements and popular misconceptions. The lesson that emerges is to be on your guard against making investment decisions on the basis of widely publicised, often repeated, incorrect statements.

Allow for possible bias from some of the statements. For example, the performance of shares compared with fixed-interest investments is often over-stated. Now, it is true that in the long term stocks have performed better than fixed-interest investments. But the margin is a good deal less than some people would suggest.

One reason is that the comparisons are generally made between stocks and long term fixed-interest investments of about 10 years. As those latter investments were affected for a good deal of the last 20 years by changes in interest rates which had an adverse effect on capital value, that fact distorts the comparison.

If the comparison is made with fixed-interest investments over a medium term of about two years, the picture is considerably different. They would still show that over a number of periods shares generally perform better, but the margin is a good deal lower.

As indicated above, that still leaves the basic situation that stocks in the medium to long term generally do better than fixed-interest investments. But, to some investors, particularly those whose situation is such that they have to be conservative, the fact that the low risk investments have done better than shares in more than a fifth of the periods, is a factor to which they might like to attach some weight.

How the ASC and the Federal Government have encouraged false information

One of the main reasons for the unsatisfactory situation in relation to information and advice provided by investment advisers is that the Australian Securities Commission (ASC) has given too much attention to the comments of the Financial Planning Association and completely, or almost completely, ignored the recommendations of the Australian Investors Association (AIA). An Issues Paper published by the ASC in February 1995 stated that the Financial Planning Association plays an active role in the development of ASC policies and practice notes.

In the investment advisory field there are two types of advisers. There are commercial advisers who derive all or most of their income from commissions. Hence, they cannot be described as independent because what they recommend or do not recommend has a big effect on the remuneration they receive. There are also professional advisers who operate on a genuine fee basis passing on all commissions to clients. The members on the Practitioner Member list of the AIA, (see Appendix A) meet that standard as well as other Association standards, concerning adequate tertiary qualifications and experience. With due respect to the many well-meaning people in the Financial Planning Association, the vast majority of their members are of the commercial type discussed above.

There is evidence to suggest that the ASC, in refusing to act on complaints by investors who had not been given adequate information by the members of the Financial Planning Association, have apparently accepted the false claim of the many financial planners that losses suffered in property trusts before 1990 and in share trusts in the 1987 crash and in the 1994 slump were not the responsibility of the advisers because those investments were popular at the time.

The question is not whether the investments were popular or not, but whether advisers met their specific obligations under the Corporations Law to disclose all material information, including full information about the extent of the risk involved.

As repeated representation to the Attorney General and the Prime Minister on this position has been fruitless, the Federal Government is also responsible. The AIA has decided that the matter should be raised with the Joint Parliamentary Committee on Corporations and Securities. It has also called for a full enquiry into the investment industry including the failure of the ASC to enforce the law effectively, the unhealthy relations between fund managers and investment advisers, the inappropriate close association between the ASC and the Financial Planning Association and other matters.

♦ *Third World Standards*

The regulatory standards in relation to enforcement of the law in Australia are far behind those in other countries such as the US, Britain and Singapore. That means that Australian investors have to be considerably more wary than investors in other countries about what fund managers and advisers tell them. In contrast to high Australian standards in so many other areas, the standards of investment regulations in this country are little, if any, better than in the most unsophisticated third world country.

Objective voices are in the minority

One of the reasons for commenting on these various fallacies is that those who more objectively analyse share market behaviour rather than going along with the conventional wisdom, tend to be very much a small minority. If, indeed, their voices were heard more frequently, then the fallacies would not be so widespread and it would not be necessary to draw so much attention to them.

Keynes said it all

Whenever I am tempted to hesitate about writing on the importance of fallacies, I am encouraged to do so by the statement of the late Lord Keynes which is referred to in an Chapter Three. He said that, in the investment business, plaudits tend to go to those who are conventionally unsuccessful rather than to those who succeed by unconventional means.

Chapter 5

Invest Directly or Through Unit Trusts and Other Types of Managed Funds?

Questions to be considered

There is an old saying that people who act as their own lawyers have fools for clients. In an age of specialisation, there may be an initial tendency to believe that unit trusts and other institutions with vast research resources and highly paid specialists must be in a far stronger position to make better investment decisions than the typical investor.

But experience shows that the answer is not nearly as simple as that. In the long term, most institutions do not do any better than the market average. So this chapter commences with looking at the question of whether it is possible for individual investors, who put their minds to it, to do better than institutions.

It proceeds to consider following issues:

➢ The advantages and disadvantages of unit trusts

➢ The significance of charges

➢ Whether past performance is a reliable indicator of the future

➢ The place of index funds

➢ Selection of unit trusts

➢ The effect of a medium term timing strategy on unit trust investment decisions

➢ An overall strategy for investors.

Can individuals do better than institutions?

The answer to that question is "yes" — provided they adopt a logical disciplined approach to stocks and follow sound investment practices including those discussed in this book. One reason for this situation is the fact referred to above, namely that most institutions do not do as well as the market average. That results to a great extent because the institutions are often not logical and disciplined, mainly because of continuing pressure from their marketing people to outperform their competitors in the short term.

It is often a case of the marketing tail wagging the investment dog. To continue the canine analogy, many institutions spend a lot of time chasing their tails in a futile attempt to be top performer every month or every three months.

The other reason is that the charges of unit trusts have a big impact on the return to the investor.

In a paper on Stock Analysis at the 1994 Annual Investor Retreat of the American Association of Individual Investors in Maui, Hawaii, Prof. C. Thomas Howard referred to the importance of fundamental analysis which:

> *"does not try to pick market peaks and troughs; rather it attempts to avoid selling undervalued stocks and avoid buying overvalued stocks"*

He went on to say that:

> *"various studies indicate that the following goals are reachable for an individual investor:*
>
> *1) Pick the correct stock 55 per cent of the time.*
>
> *2) Beat the market by 2 per cent to 3 per cent.*
>
> *3) Avoid being a noise trader ....*
>
> *"Noise is the result of non-information based trades; that is, trades driven by other than fundamental economic and financial information".*

What are unit trusts?

Unit trusts are funds operated by investment companies. They raise money from investors and invest it in stocks, bonds, money market securities, options and commodities. It is primarily the trusts invested in shares which are the subject of this chapter.

There are various types of unit trusts which vary from those which offer the prospects of low income — but very high capital gain, if all goes well, with high risk — to those which offer prospects of a relatively high income with only moderate capital gain and relatively low risk. There are also unit trusts which invest in specific industries, or national markets or types of stocks such as small companies' trusts.

As indicated in Chapter Four, the use of the term "growth" (in relation to "growth stocks"), is often a case of a misleading label and the terms "variable" or "very variable" would be more appropriate.

In the bond funds, the prospects of capital gain and risk of capital loss are affected by the length of time to maturity of the bonds in the portfolio. Many bond funds, especially with a portfolio with a long average period to maturity, fared badly in 1994.

The international funds can produce much higher capital gains or much higher capital losses than funds invested in Australian stocks because of fluctuations in currency values.

Advantages of Unit Trusts

The main advantages of unit trusts are:

➢ **Broad diversification** — a wide spread of funds over different stocks which reduces the specific risk, e.g. of a disaster striking one company but not the major systemic risk, namely the risk of an overall market decline.

➢ **Professional management**

➢ **Liquidity** — the ability of investors to sell their units back at any time. This advantage is also enjoyed by investors in shares which are listed on major exchanges and enjoy active trading.

➢ **Convenience** — There is a good deal less record-keeping for one investment in a unit trust than if the same amount of capital were invested in a number of separate stocks.

Disadvantages of Unit Trusts

The main disadvantages of unit trusts are:

➤ **Loss of control** — In a unit trust, investors are no longer masters of their own destinies in that decisions on what to buy, whether to sell, and so on, are made by the mutual fund managers. There is also the loss of the personal relationship with advisers.

➤ **Costs** — The various costs, especially of some unit trusts, can be large. This is discussed below.

➤ **Possible tax disadvantages** — Investors in unit trusts cannot control the realisation of capital gains, for example, to realise gains to offset against losses which have been realised on other investments. Though individuals prefer to plan on the basis of after-tax results, most unit trusts, partly because of marketing pressures, tend to plan on a before tax basis.

➤ **Vast diversity of funds** — The number of trusts and managed funds has grown to several hundred which makes the selection of the most appropriate fund a major task. Investors with limited sales resistance could end up with a very large number of different mutual fund investments and a very unwieldy portfolio. This could negate the advantage of convenience discussed above.

➤ **Performance** — The performance of many unit trusts and other managed funds has been disappointing and inconsistent.

Unit trust charges

Investment in the majority of trusts involves two types of charges. First, there is a "load" that pays for the sales force and second, periodical management charges plus some fund administration expenses. In "no load" funds, there is only the latter type of charges.

The load may be an entry fee of up to 5 per cent of the initial investment or an exit fee of the same range, payable on sale of the investment.

The management fees and the other fees and charges, such as custodial and legal fees, range from about 1.75 per cent to 2.5 per cent per annum.

Brokerage costs on purchases and sales of shares in the portfolio of the fund vary depending on degree of activity.

◆ *Costs in relation to income*

If the annual expenses are related to income rather than to assets, the ratio would be up to 75 per cent in many cases. The point was made earlier that if share prices had increased above the 1994 peak, as many investment people were suggesting, the consequent reduction in dividend yield could mean that the income of some share funds would be less than the annual expenses. So investors would then receive a debit note for the difference rather than a dividend.

Investors need to remember that in addition to the reduction of income due to annual charges, the impact of any front load also lowers the net return to investors, because for each $100 they invest only $95 or $96 goes into stocks.

The significance of charges and low cost funds

The full impact of charges on investment return is not widely understood by the investing public. For example, an annual expense rate of 2.5 per cent may seem to be a small impost at first sight. Moreover, at times of a rapidly rising market when unit trust prices are rising 10 per cent or 20 per cent or more per annum, (the time when many people are persuaded to invest in unit trusts) it may appear negligible. But in the longer term, when total return from income and capital gain is in the 11 per cent to 12 per cent per annum range, it becomes very significant. It can be even more significant for those many unit trust and other managed funds in which the investment performance is below the market average.

In *Bogle on Mutual Funds*, (Richard D. Irwin Inc. 1994) John Bogle, founder and CEO of the Vanguard Investment Group, demonstrates the effect this way (p. 191):

"If a stock fund earns a gross return of +12 %, the fund's net return will be 11.4%, if it incurs annual expenses of 0.6%. But the fund's net return will be +9.5% if it incurs expenses of 2.5%. A return of +11.4% provides 20% more dollars than a return of 9.5% in one year and 31% more dollars over ten years."

As for entry charges, the claim that is put forward by some fund managers and brokers is that funds with entry charges have better performances. John Bogle's comment on that point is (p.196):

"But there is absolutely no evidence that the returns on stock funds that charge a load are sufficient to overcome the drag of their sales charges. It seems unlikely that it could happen, unless the existence of a sales force somehow endows a portfolio manager with superior stock picking ability — a far fetched notion."

♦ *Low cost funds*

It is clear, then, that investors who have decided that part of their capital is to be invested in unit trusts should look for the low cost unit trust or other managed funds.

Unfortunately, there are not many no load or low load managed funds in Australia. Some of the rollover and allocated pensions offer no entry and no exit fees. The GT Group offers on their Australian and overseas trusts no entry fee with no exit fee after five years and an exit fee reducing from 5 per cent to nil over five years. The lowest annual charge for management fees and expenses is about 1.7 per cent compound with 0.3 per cent in some US funds.

The unique Vanguard Group situation

This US group was founded by John Bogle, author of *Bogle on Mutual Funds* which is referred to earlier in this chapter. A leader in the mutual fund industry, he is a crusader for the rights of investors and an outspoken critic of unfair treatment of mutual fund investors.

His book criticises the lack of adequate disclosure, by fund managers, of the impact of charges on investors. It describes how advertisements are often misleading in selectively quoting results for periods favourable to the managers while failing to disclose vastly different results in other periods. It also discusses how investors can get more reliable information about mutual funds and the need for investors to demand more candour from managers.

The Vanguard Group of investment companies which he founded in 1974, and of which he is Chairman and Chief Executive Officer, has a structure which is unique in the mutual fund industry. The funds own all of the stock in the Vanguard Group Incorporated which provides essential services — management, investment and distribution — on an at cost basis.

This situation is probably the main reason for the charges of Vanguard funds being so much below the industry average. All of the funds are no load funds. The expense ratio for bond funds is as low as about 0.2 per cent and for stock funds about 0.5 per cent.

Australian investors who wish to invest in overseas shares who are aware of and can afford to face additional risk of currency fluctuations, may be interested in the funds of this Group. They would need to remember that if the capital of an investor and associates in overseas investments exceeds $50,000, Australian tax is payable on unrealised capital gain.

The Vanguard funds are index funds (which are described in the next section). The address of The Vanguard Group of Investment Companies is Post Office Box 2600, Valley Forge, Pennsylvania 19482-2600.

Past performance may not indicate future results

One of the most serious problems for investors in selecting mutual funds is that past performance, generally, is not a reliable indicator of future results. The problem is compounded by excessive attention in advertisements, in the financial media, and in performance surveys to very short term results over three months to one year.

Those figures can be grossly misleading. Moreover, competitive pressures on fund managers to outperform competitors in such short periods means that many of them fail to have the discipline and the mental courage to stay with medium to long term strategies which are the essence of any sound investment programme.

Even for longer periods, past performance is generally not a good indicator of future results. Figures on page 88 of *Bogle on Mutual Funds,* (the book cited above,) for two successive ten year periods are extremely interesting.

The average rank of the top 20 unit trust performers in one decade was 142 out of 309 in the next decade. In terms of statistical significance, that is little different from what may be expected at random. Only four of the top 20 funds in the first decade remained in the top 20 in the second.

Index funds

Index unit trusts or managed funds are funds in which the portfolios match a market index such as the All Ordinaries and the results should match the results for the overall market. Low cost index funds without any load and with low management fees should produce results very close to the overall market. But for index funds with loads and annual management fees the results could be below the overall market by 2 per cent to 3 per cent, or more.

In Chapter Nine of *Bogle on Mutual Funds,* the subject of index funds is covered at length. John Bogle and his Vanguard Group are firm supporters of the index fund concept.

The argument for index funds is basically that not many fund managers do better than the overall market and it is difficult to select those managers in advance. This is especially so after allowing for total fund charges. So, the argument goes, it is better to invest in an index fund as the long term results, before charges, should be about the same as for active funds and better when charges are taken into account.

Costs to the investor in index funds, sometimes called passive funds, are generally lower than for active funds — both the management charges and the costs of brokerage are lower than for active funds in which there may be a great deal of purchases and sales of stocks in the pursuit of better results.

"Therefore, you should invest only in those index funds with the lowest expense ratios," writes John Bogle, *"and you should never pay a sales charge when you invest in an index fund"*.

Unfortunately, there are no Australian index funds with no load or low load annual charges.

The Index fund of the Australian Trust managed by the MLC Group has an entry fee of 5 per cent and annual charges of about 1.6 per cent per annum.

John Bogle points out that the index fund concept is based on the efficient market hypothesis. But it has been stated earlier that the credibility of that hypothesis has been severely damaged by:

➤ The points made by behavioural finance people including Professor R. Shiller.

➤ Rejection by highly respected practitioners such as Warren Buffett, George Soros and others quoted in *The Midas Touch* by John Train.

➤ Repeated examples of gross market inefficiency including the October 1987 stock market crash, and anomalies on certain days and months.

➤ Unrealistic assumptions in the capital asset pricing model, including the fallacy that most investors are risk averse which are discussed in Chapter Four.

➤ The evidence quoted in Chapter One showing that medium term timing pays off and that vastly better results have been achieved by investing when the stock market is in or near Zones 4 or 5 rather than when it is in Zones 1 or 2.

For those reasons, I believe that better results will be achieved by the realistic investment philosophy and medium term timing outlined in Chapter One and discussed at greater length in later chapters.

But, it is true that for people who do not wish to undertake the processes in medium term timing and selection of stocks for investment, low cost index funds should produce a better net result to investors, after allowing for charges, than most active funds.

♦ *Index funds and other approaches*

Some investors may decide to place a portion of their capital in a low cost index fund to achieve better results than in most active funds, while investing the remainder of the common stock portion of their portfolio in stocks using the principles of realistic investing and stock selection described in this book.

Others who accept the merits of realistic investment discussed in this book but who do not wish to be involved in stock selection for all or part of their capital, may use the medium term timing techniques to time moves into or out of index funds. On the basis of past experience discussed in Chapter One, that should produce better results with lower downside risk than being in index funds all of the time.

Unit trusts, market risk and medium term timing

Many of the comments in advertisements for unit trusts, in their annual reports and in recommendations of advisers, imply that the diversification provided by the funds protects investors against all investment risk. That is not true because diversification is no protection against the risk of a major decline in the overall market. So there is a risk of a capital decline of up to 40 per cent or more in a market slump, with complete recovery taking up to several years. Investors in equity trusts also need to remember the other point made earlier in the text that there have been periods of up to 15 years when the overall share market has produced little or no sustained gain.

There is also little or no truth in the claim that the investment expertise of the managers will produce good results or protect the invested capital from loss. Most managers do not do any better than the market average.

The other important point to remember is that medium term timing of purchases and sales of equity trusts is just as important as it is for direct investment in stocks. Indeed, the risk is greater, especially in funds with loads. The combination of loads, and management fees can greatly increase the loss in a market slump. For example, a decline of 10 per cent in the market, soon after investment could mean that a unit trust investor could be facing a total capital decline of up to 15 per cent or 17 per cent.

That point further underlines the benefit of investing in no load funds.

Remember that there is *no* truth in the claims of some unit trust managers that timing of purchases and sales does not matter. There is a vast difference between the five year results achieved by those who invested in equity trusts in 1982 just before the boom started and sold in September 1987 just before the crash, compared with those who bought in September 1987 and sold in 1992.

Making specific buying and selling decisions

♦ *General principles*

Any purchases or sales of unit trusts should be within the framework of:

➢ **Policy** — The policy decision of individual investors as to what portion of their capital should be exposed to stock market risk, as part of their semi-permanent investment policy.

➢ **Timing** — Timing decisions based on the principles of realistic investing and medium term timing referred to above and elsewhere in this book. Those factors enable investors to decide whether at a particular time share investments should be moving to the upper limit of their policy range (for example between zero and 60 per cent), or towards the lower limit or somewhere in between.

➢ **Shares or funds** — The extent to which the common share component of the portfolio is to be invested directly in stocks or indirectly through mutual funds.

➢ **Spread** — The need for some spread over different management groups as a protection against performance risk, namely the risk that the managers with above average performance in the past may not maintain that position.

➢ **Costs** — The crucial importance of fees and charges. In the long run, performance of fund managers tends to regress to the mean (or in other words the better performances tend to come back to the average). So the difference in the long term net return to investors is often due to the level of costs which tends to make no load funds with low management charges attractive.

➢ **Family of funds** — Other things being equal, it may be wise to invest in a unit trust which is part of a family of funds of various types in which funds may be switched from one type to another with little or no cost.

➢ **Suitable type** — Before considering specific funds, make a decision on the type of fund which is appropriate to your present situation and the current composition of your portfolio. Subject to current portfolio situation and overall policy considerations balanced funds would be more suitable to retired people or others with little or no income from other sources. Younger and middle aged people with adequate income, who can afford to face higher risk, may prefer the "growth" funds.

♦ *Consideration of specific funds*

After considering all of the above factors, a decision on the funds in which you wish to invest comes down to finding funds which meet these standards:

➢ Low charges

➢ A reasonably good investment performance for the fund in which you are interested and for all of the funds managed by the management group

➢ A management group which appears to be reasonably professional in its approach, as distinct from some with aggressive marketing approaches

➢ Funds and managers whose performances in periods of severe market slump are relatively good.

Remember the comments earlier in the chapter about the fact that funds with superior performances in one period, for even as long as ten years, may be considerably less impressive in following periods. Though even long term performance is not necessarily a reliable guide to the future, it is essential to look at performance figures for several years, e.g. five or seven, rather than for short periods such as a few months or a year which, unfortunately, are the subject of so much media comment.

Performances should be compared with both relevant market indices and industry average performance for that type of mutual fund. Remember that some published performance figures do not allow for all costs and charges. So it may be necessary to adjust for them.

◆ *Beware the high flyers*

Experience suggests it may be unwise to invest in funds which report spectacularly good results, way ahead of their competitors in boom conditions after the stock market has been rising sharply for some time. When the crunch comes and the boom inevitably turns into a slump, those funds tend to fall from the top of the performance list to the bottom.

Their extremely good results in the boom were generally achieved by accepting well above normal risk which leads to more severe falls in the slump. This is an illustration of the workings of the hangover analogy — just as the longer the wining and dining proceeds, the worse may be the hangover next morning, so the more extreme the good results in a particular stock or unit trusts or the overall market, the more severe and prolonged the following slump is likely to be.

Sources of information on unit trusts and managed funds

◆ *Need for caution*

A good deal of the information in unit trust and managed fund prospectuses is unreliable and much of it can be misleading. So too can comments by most commissions-based advisers. The problem is that most of that information contains fallacies that have been discussed in earlier chapters. Most of the comments on the alleged superior performance of managers is a long way from the reality discussed in this chapter, in relation to the share market.

Understanding Unit Trusts — A Guide for Australian Investors, Charles Beelaerts and Kevin Forde (Wrightbooks, Melbourne, 1994) contains a good deal of useful information on this subject.

Money Management: This fortnightly investment industry newspaper publishes performance figures for up to three years for unit trusts, investment bonds, rollovers, and superannuation funds. The figures are in about 30 different categories. For one, two and three years the figures show the amount to which $1,000 would have grown. They also show the ranking of each product compared with others in that category. Those latter figures are after allowing for annual management charges but do not allow for entry or exit fees. So to arrive at the net return for investors the figures would have to be reduced by up to 5 per cent.

The Age: This Melbourne newspaper publishes each Monday the one and three year earning rates, after allowing for entry and exit fees.

♦ *Other publications*

Articles on various aspects of unit trusts and managed funds appear from time to time in the financial press, and in magazines such as *Personal Investment* and *Business Review Weekly*.

For those interested in investing in US mutual funds the following publications may be helpful:

➤ *Forbes*: Forbes Inc., 60 Fifth Avenue, New York, N.Y. 10011; (800) 888-9896 (biweekly). Every year, one of the issues (August or September) gives statistics and ratings of mutual funds.

➤ *The Handbook for No-Load Fund Investors*: The No-Load Fund Investor, Inc., P.O. Box 318, Irvington-on-Hudson, N.Y. 10533; (914) 693-7420 (annual). Provides an explanation of how to invest in mutual funds. In addition, it contains chapters and tables of mutual fund performance, and it provides a directory of 1,700 no-load funds.

➤ *The Individual Investor's Guide to Low-Load Mutual Funds*: American Association of Individual Investors, 625

N. Michigan Avenue, Suite 1900, Chicago, Ill. 60611;
(312) 280-0170 (annual). All AAII members receive a
comprehensive book with a detailed analysis of low-load
mutual funds, including their historical performance, a
statistical summary, fund objectives and services, the name
of the portfolio manager, fund addresses and telephone
numbers, and strategies for effective mutual fund investing.
(The Low-Load Guide is published annually in March. It is
free to members and $19 for each additional member copy;
the non-member price is $24.95.)

Other types of managed funds

Most of the comments in this chapter would also apply, not
only to unit trusts but to other types of managed funds which
invest in shares. They include investment bonds offered by life
insurance companies and friendly societies, superannuation
funds, rollover products, allocated pensions.

Summary

Unit trusts and other managed funds may be helpful for some
investors. But the vast majority of share investors would
generally be better off investing directly.

Chapter 6

A Policy for
Each Individual and
Strategies for
Changing Times

One of the very best reasons you can have for not making a particular investment is that you cannot afford it. Nobody would challenge the logic of that statement. But the investments made by many people over the years which cause considerable financial distress to them ignored that basic principle.

Generally, it was not that the investors themselves were reckless or foolhardy. Mostly, when they went into investments with a far higher risk than they could afford to face it was because they were not aware of that risk. Frequently, they were victims of the RCs — the risk concealers. They were victims of the old fallacies, mainly that you can't go wrong in blue chip stocks.

High risk portfolios by default

In reviewing portfolios of conservative people who have told me that they do not wish to face a high degree of risk, I often find that they have in fact a relatively high risk portfolio. A significant part of the capital is in the medium risk area such as shares, or higher risk investments including negative gearing and more risky shares such as mineral exploration companies or new ventures.

Obviously they did not set a policy to go into high risk investments. They drifted into them more or less by default because they had never considered the need for an investment policy and the people who advised them on investments had not pointed out the importance of this essential step to success in investment. So the higher risk investments just happened primarily because at the time they were investing the medium and high risk investments happened to be flavour of the month.

The need for a sound policy

In most activities we need to make decisions that are based on a sound policy rather than make a series of decisions which have no cohesion, no real relation to each other. In the investment area, where the whole of investors' life savings may be at stake, the need for a sound policy is even more important.

So before you make decisions as to how much of your capital should go into the stock market or whether you should buy or sell any particular stock, you need to follow a first-things-first approach of deciding on the basic policy.

Factors that affect policy

Though policies need to be suitable for the varying requirements of individual investors, there are a few basic factors to be considered:

◆ *Age*

In general, older investors need and tend to prefer a more conservative policy than would be suitable for younger people. As they have built up their life savings through hard work over a period of years they need a fair degree of emphasis on stability and safety. They would not wish to expose that capital to undue risk.

◆ *Retired people*

Retired people generally need to follow a low risk policy. Because they are no longer earning income, they do not have the opportunity, which is available to younger people, of rebuilding their capital after any investment market reverse out of savings from career earnings.

◆ *Income from other sources*

As well as retired people there are other people such as widows or invalids or disabled people who have to depend on their investments for all of their income (with the possible exception of some contribution from a pension). Hence, there is a need for them to follow a lower risk policy than would be appropriate for other people.

By contrast, those who have adequate income from a salary, business or profession, can afford a higher risk policy which would expose a greater portion of their capital to market risk.

Obviously, investors with a large amount of capital available can generally adopt a more venturesome or less conservative policy than those with a smaller amount of capital. The reason is that even if they suffer a severe loss in markets, for example in stock markets and property markets which both went into a severe slump at the same time in 1974 and other periods in the past, it would not be disastrous.

◆ *Future cash needs*

Investors who need a significant amount of cash in the next few years to buy a business or a home or for an extended overseas trip, or any other purpose, need a lower risk policy. The reason is that the time when it is necessary for them to turn part of their investments into cash could happen to coincide with a weak point in investment markets. So they would need to have a relatively large proportion of their capital in investments which are not subject to fluctuation.

◆ *Attitude to risk*

In addition to the above more or less objective items there is the subject of the psychological matter of attitude to risk. Consider two investors whose situation in regard to the other attributes discussed above is identical. But one is a person who, because of business experience or other factors doesn't worry unduly about problems. The other person is what some people call a "born worrier" — a person who worries and frets about problems.

The latter person would need to place a larger proportion of his capital in the lower risk investments which are not subject to market fluctuation than the former. It is important to remember that even for share investments which do very well over the medium to long term, there can be periods of up to several years when they are in decline. The strain which that situation would put on the "born worrier" type of person could affect his well being and even his health.

For that person, logical reasons may suggest a medium risk policy but important psychological consideration could indicate a lower risk policy. These factors are particularly relevant for retired people for the simple reason that if they are retired they have a lot more time to worry about things than in earlier years when their job or their business or their family responsibilities kept them a lot busier.

Taxation and investment policy

Obviously, taxation has to be considered in proper perspective in relation to setting an investment policy. This matter is discussed in Chapter Seven.

Policy ranges for different types of investors

In considering an investment policy, the key decision is the degree to which the capital will be exposed to risk. This calls for considering the reality of market risk, not the conventional wisdom and the investment platitudes that "you can't go wrong in so called blue chips", or that "any declines in stock market values are likely to be relatively small and not last very long".

Let us consider two extremes. First a retired couple with modest capital in the range of about $100,000 to $250,000 with no income from other sources other than a small pension. The other is a middle aged person with a high income that is more than adequate to meet living expenses and a capital of $500,000 or more available for investment (excluding capital tied up in the family home).

It is obvious from the comments above that the latter person could afford to have a considerable portion of his or her capital in medium risk investments which are exposed to the risk of market fluctuation. (Medium risk investments are those such as shares or property where market fluctuations can cause a loss of 40 per cent of capital or more. Low risk investments are short to medium term government stock, bank deposits or bonds in sound companies where investors know they will receive a definite amount of income each quarter or half year and that the capital will be repaid on a specified date.)

Some would argue that such a person could afford to have the whole of his or her capital in a medium risk area with part of it in the higher risk investments such as negative gearing, commodities, futures trading, options trading, etc. But even for investors with a large amount of capital and a large income from other sources there is a need to have portions of capital in what could be called a "fail safe" component of low risk investments. That would mean that some would be "out of harms way" in the event of both share and property markets declining by 40 per cent or more at the same time.

So a policy for investors in that situation could be to have a minimum of 25 per cent in the low risk investments. This would mean that they could have up to 75 per cent in the medium and high risk investments. The portion in low risk investments can help them to be more successful in stocks or other medium risk investments. If there is a need for cash when the stock market is in a slump, the portion of capital in low risk investments can be used. This eliminates the need to sell stock at unfavourable prices.

The former investor, the retired person with limited capital and no other income, cannot afford to place much capital in medium risk areas where it is exposed to significant market fluctuation. So a reasonable portion for this investor could be a maximum of 10 per cent to 25 per cent in a medium risk area with the balance in the low risk area. They are not in a position to seek possible capital gain and tax benefits on a large part of their capital because they need a high degree of stability of both capital and income.

So for these investors who are at the two different extremes, policy considerations would suggest that for the retired people of limited means a suitable policy would be as under.

Risk Category of Investments	Minimum (%)	Maximum (%)
High	0	0
Medium	0	25
Low	75	100

On the other hand, for the better off investors with a large amount of capital and income, the policy ranges could be as shown in the following table.

Risk Category of Investments	Minimum (%)	Maximum (%)
High	0	15
Medium	25	75
Low	25	75

If necessary the policy allocation could be refined. For example, in the case of the latter investors, i.e. the better off investors, the policy may include a sum for investment in high risk investments listed earlier for which policy ranges of zero to 15 per cent may be appropriate. In that event it is important to note that the total at any time in the medium plus high risk investments should not exceed the 75 per cent so that there is the figure of 25 per cent in "fail safe" component of the portfolio.

Investors who are in a position somewhere between those two extremes could find policy ranges in some intermediate position.

The suggested ranges above are the policy ranges which should be a semi-permanent feature of the policy of the investor and be subject to change only when the situation of the investor alters considerably. The question of possible changes to meet changing market conditions is discussed below.

Strategy for current conditions

Because market conditions change so much and timing is such a crucial part of investment in the medium and high risk area, the amount committed to those areas should vary depending on the assessment of current market trends.

For example, for the better off investors the policy range in the medium risk investments is zero to 75 per cent. There are times when indicators are very favourable with stock prices below their long term trend, stock prices are relatively cheap on the basis of dividend yields compared with interest rates and the cyclical position is favourable because the market shows signs of recovery after bouncing along the bottom for some time in a slump. In those conditions, the aim would be to have the portion in the medium risk area (including stocks) move up towards the maximum figure of 75 per cent.

In opposite conditions, the amount in stocks would be moved down towards the lower limit of 25 per cent.

That sort of approach would be adopted by various investors with different policy ranges. One of the great advantages of stock investment is that it is possible to increase or reduce the holding in the overall market, in particular segments of the market, or in individual stocks in small steps by selling or buying an amount that may be 5 per cent or 10 per cent, or whatever, of total capital. Use of that approach in the step system ensures that the amount in stocks at any time is within the policy range for the individual, with the percentage allocated to stocks being determined according to an assessment of current market conditions.

Practical advantages

Apart from being the only logical basis for making investment decisions, there are significant practical advantages to this approach. The investor who uses this approach knows that he has invested in areas outside the market not subject to risk of market fluctuation, an amount that is appropriate for his policy situation and for the assessment of current market conditions.

So if he wishes to take advantage of special situations he can do so with a good deal more confidence. By way of a rough analogy he is like the prudent punter at the races who takes to the track only the amount of money which he is prepared to lose. He knows that if a severe market slump occurs suddenly the loss to which he is likely to be exposed is reasonable in relation to his overall situation.

Importance of portfolio effect

As part of the sensible approach of considering policy and strategy or timing factors, the other important matter is the consideration in all investment decisions of the effect on the overall portfolio. Any buy or sell decision must be made in the context the whole portfolio.

For example, a soundly based recommendation to invest in a particular stock which looks attractive, may not be a wise decision if it involves the total amount invested in stocks going over what is a reasonable proportion of capital, on the basis of these policy and strategy considerations.

If the stock which has been recommended is attractive, but a purchase would produce an overall portfolio effect which would seem to be unwise, then the next question is whether it would be better to sell part of the existing holding so that the special situation of the stock being recommended could be purchased within overall policy and strategy considerations.

Policy and strategy considerations within the share component of the overall portfolio

There are some policy and strategy considerations which are relevant in looking at the composition of the share component of the overall portfolio. If all stocks had the same risk characteristics, this would not be so relevant. But the fact is that there can be significant differences in the risk characteristics of different stocks.

When this point is being discussed there is a tendency to feel, correctly, that mineral exploration stocks and stocks in new ventures should be considered more risky than others. Another factor which is not so apparent, and goes completely contrary to the conventional wisdom, is that it is also necessary to recognise the following facts:

➤ The leading stocks, the so called blue chips, the quality stocks, the favourite "growth" stocks are generally more risky than other less prestigious stocks.

➤ Stocks which are attractively priced, i.e. providing a dividend yield above the average with the dividend reasonably well covered by earnings and good prospects are less risky than more popular highly recommended stocks producing lower dividend yields. The reason is that in a stock market decline the former stock would reach a level where the increased dividend yield, as the result of the lower prices, could tend to attract buying support. But at that stage the "tall poppy" stocks, even with the lower prices, would still be on yields which would be very unattractive in the more sober assessment that always occurs in slumps.

➢ Remember the harsh reality that despite all the hype to the contrary there are really no such things as good stocks and bad stocks — just some stocks which have a good probability of increasing and others with a good probability of price decreases.

➢ A "good stock", which has produced good earnings, dividends and capital gains in the past, reaches a stage where it is a more risky investment than other stocks with less spectacular records because a sharp reaction to excessive market enthusiasm in the past could push the prices of the "good" stock down further.

Policy on types of investment with greater risk

As indicated, general discussions on policy apply to the overall stock market situation. It is necessary, then, to consider the realities of risk including the factors discussed above.

There are share investments which involve a higher degree of risk than normal. Investing in international stocks where there is a dual risk of currency fluctuation and stock market fluctuation is one example. Trading in options or stock market futures in another. Buying stocks for benefits through negative gearing also involves higher risk. In some of these investments there is a risk that investors can lose more than 100 per cent of their capital.

Because those investments are not in the medium risk category but in the higher risk category, policy considerations would generally require a much smaller portion of capital be invested in that area than in the stock market generally.

Revision of policy and strategy

To a considerable extent, policies should be set for the relatively long term. For retired people, for example, a policy they set at the age of 65, or when they retire, is likely to be the policy which they will follow for the rest of their lives.

The policy should certainly be reviewed when there is a significant change in the position of investors. Investors would generally feel it reasonable to expose their capital to a somewhat higher degree of risk when their children have grown up and are no longer financially dependent on them. In the situation where one spouse, who has not been earning income in the past, commences to earn income and expects to continue to do so, that would be another situation when a policy could be revised to a somewhat more risky stance. Investors moving from a situation of secure employment, on a salary basis, to commencing their own business would generally find a more conservative policy appropriate. This would be especially true if they were in a business where there was a more than normal business risk.

Those investors whose main activities are exposed to a great deal of risk, for example farmers, who face droughts, natural disasters and gyrations of the world commodity markets, would generally need to have a more defensive policy with a smaller portion of the capital exposed to market fluctuation than those in more stable businesses.

Chapter 7

A Balanced Approach
to Tax and Means
Test Considerations

A sale, according to a cynical definition, is what many people attend to save more money than they can really afford. By the same token you could say that some investors seek more taxation benefits than they can really afford.

Sharing a profit with the Tax or Social Security Department may be wise

It is often better to share a profit with the Taxation Department than to have a loss all to yourself later on. Though none of us like paying tax, we have to make sure that the taxation tail does not wag the sound investment dog in our decision-making process.

There are examples of many people who suffered severely losing large parts of their capital, from investment in so called growth stocks or unit trusts, in an attempt to gain the major part of their return by way of capital gain rather than income. These are people who refrain from making precautionary sales of stocks when a slump is imminent because they place too much emphasis on the tax they would pay rather than on the net profit after tax which they would achieve.

Dividend tax credit

The tax credit on dividends, and the fact that this component of return on shares is not taken into account in the Means Test, have some appeal. But that must be balanced against the fact that shares are medium risk investments in which most retired people should not invest heavily. Moreover, unless they have a significant amount of taxable income from other sources, including fixed-interest or unfranked dividend income, they may waste some of the dividend tax credit.

This is relevant to investors whose marginal tax rate is below the tax credit rate of 33 per cent. That would include a large number of retired couples with a combined investment income of about $40,000. For them, investing a significant amount of their capital in the low risk fixed-interest area in the interests of safety, also ensures that any tax credit on dividend income will not be wasted.

Excessive promotion of tax and benefits

One of the reasons for people making unwise decisions by ignoring the above comments, is that tax benefits are so heavily promoted by investment advisers, fund managers and others. A lot of money has been made by those people as the result of exaggerating the tax benefits which investments produce.

Do the tax benefits justify a higher risk?

Almost inevitably, the investments which may offer tax or Means Test benefits involve a higher degree of risk. Stocks which can provide dividend tax credits and benefits on taxation of capital gain, because the inflation component is not taxed, are a medium risk investment because of the significant market fluctuations. Market fluctuations also make property and many other types of investments more risky than investments which provide an assured return and repayment of capital on the specified date.

So the taxation or Means Test benefits should be considered in the same way as any another benefits expected from investments — i.e. are all the benefits, including any taxation benefits, reasonable in relation to the risk involved? Even if there is an attractive benefits-to-risk relationship, is the risk involved one which that particular investor can afford to face after considering the overall risk of his portfolio? Those are the questions which need to be considered in a rational balanced approach to taxation benefits.

Are marginal or average tax rates relevant

Advisers, fund managers and some stockbrokers, in emphasising the tax benefits in relation to capital gain on share investments invariably use the marginal tax rate. For many decisions that is the relevant rate to be used.

For example consider a married couple with a taxable income of $30,000, i.e. $15,000 each, where the marginal tax rate including Medicare is 21.4 per cent. If an investment increases that income by $10,000, i.e. $5000 each, their total tax will increase by $2140. So the marginal tax rate of 21.4 per cent is relevant.

But in a situation of a person who has no other income and has an amount for investment which will produce an income of $20,000, the tax impact would be much less than 21.4 per cent. The tax free threshold and the pensioner rebate would *reduce* the tax impact.

Maximising benefits from superannuation

Though going into an investment solely because of tax benefits is not sound, it is wise as part of overall investment and tax planning, to make maximum use of tax benefits in superannuation. It may help to place those investments which produce relatively high taxable income in the tax advantaged plans — subject to a thorough consideration of those complex matters.

The elements of a balanced approach to taxation and Means Test

The comments in this chapter on possible taxation and Means Test benefits of share investments (or of other investments) and the need for a balanced approach could be summarised as under:

➤ **Are investments comparable?** — If there are two investments which are comparable or close to comparable, one of which offers tax benefits then normally that investment would be preferable.

➤ **Investment merits** — Consider any proposed investment on its investment merits first. Then consider any tax benefits.

➤ **Risk versus benefits** — It is absolutely essential, when seeking any tax benefits, to weigh up the risk involved (including risk of market fluctuation), against any benefits that may be achieved.

➤ **Illusory benefits** — Remember that some tax benefits are illusory rather than real. For example, consider the so called tax-free portion of income distributions of some top property trusts which really represent a part return of capital because the cost of depreciation has not been brought to account.

Beware of possible tax traps in unit trusts

You need to be aware of the tax disadvantages, under certain circumstances, of large distributions of capital gains. These were discussed among the disadvantages of unit trusts in Chapter Five.

Another point is that in calculating capital gains on redemption, the total of any reinvestment of dividends or capital gains distribution must be deducted from the change in value over the period for which the investments were held. Tax on those items has already been paid. So that step is necessary to avoid paying tax twice.

Possible changes to tax legislation and need for independent advice

Changes to the Means Test, to the tax rates or to other parts of the tax law made in May each year in the Federal Budget, or at other times, could affect the matters discussed in this chapter. Moreover, because these matters can be complex, investors should seek qualified independent advice.

Chapter 8

Constructing
and Reviewing
a Portfolio

Many of the portfolios I have reviewed over the last 40 years have just "grown like Topsy". On a number of standards — such as total amount of the share portfolio, the type of shares or unit trusts in the portfolio, the number of stocks, overall suitability — they tend to be deficient. This is not surprising, because of the millions of words that have been written about why it is a good idea to buy particular stocks. But in general, investors have received very little guidance from stockbrokers or investment advisers on three very crucial factors, namely:

➤ A definite policy for the individual

➤ Timing based on strategy considerations

➤ All decisions should be made not solely on the alleged merits of particular stocks but on the impact on the overall portfolio.

The hallmarks of an ideal share portfolio

An ideal share portfolio should display the following features:

➤ It should be *appropriate* to the policy needs of the individual investor, based on such factors as amount of capital, amount of income available from other sources, likely cash needs during the next few years and attitude to risk-taking.

➤ It should be *timely* in relation to the realities of stock market trends, as to the amount exposed to stock market risk at that time.

➤ It should *minimise risk* by a spread over a number of different stocks which are not exposed to the same type of business risk.

➤ It should be *manageable,* which means that the number of stocks should be kept to a reasonable limit.

Basic principles of constructing and reviewing a portfolio

To construct a portfolio which aims to achieve the goals set above calls for the following:

◆ *Policy limits*

The maximum percentage of total capital available for investment to be committed to the stock market as a continuing semi-permanent policy must be decided upon. This involves a consideration of the factors discussed in Chapter Six.

◆ *Timing and strategy*

After assessing current market trends, a decision on whether the strategy for the present should be to have the stock component closer to the maximum percentage in the policy range or the minimum, or somewhere in between. This is of crucial importance in stock investments.

◆ *Reserve for special situations*

It is generally prudent to keep a reserve of somewhere between 10 per cent and 20 per cent of this total to go into the stock market to take care of special situations — for example, some new share issues which may produce well above average gains.

◆ *Number of stocks*

Decide on the approximate number of stocks in the portfolio. This involves a number which is large enough to reduce risk through a reasonable spread over different companies in different industries but which is yet small enough to manage easily — generally for individual investors about six to ten is the appropriate number.

◆ *Average amount per stock*

By dividing the number of stocks in the portfolio into the amount to be invested, after placing some capital aside for special situations, you arrive at the approximate average amount to be invested in each stock.

◆ *Maximum and minimum per stock*

Generally, somewhere about twice the average amount would be appropriate for the maximum amount per stock and about half the average amount for the minimum amount per stock. The idea would be to place an above average amount in the stocks which seem to show better than average prospects compared to the others, and a below average amount in stocks whose prospects may not be quite as good as the others.

The maximum figure serves the role of ensuring that enthusiasm does not result in placing too much in any one stock, unless there are extraordinary circumstances to warrant that decision. The minimum amount is a protection against a trap into which many investors fall, that is of having a large number of individual stocks which represent a tiny percentage of the total capital, which tend to clutter up the portfolio and make management less effective.

◆ *Dividend reinvestment*

As part of the principle of constructing and reviewing a portfolio, a firm decision should be made not to go into dividend reinvestment schemes. Although these schemes are fairly popular, they are not based on sound considerations. To go into a dividend reinvestment scheme is in effect giving a blank cheque to the company to invest an amount for you at a date six months, or eighteen months or ten years into the future, in stocks at an unknown price and in conditions which are, at the time of making that decision, completely unknown.

The apparent cost advantage of being able to buy the stocks without brokerage, and sometimes at a small discount below market price, is an illusion. Many investors have found to their sorrow when they sold stocks, that the accounting fees of making 10 or 20 or 30 separate calculations for capital gains tax purposes offset any apparent cost advantages.

An example of constructing a portfolio

Let us consider an example of a person with capital to invest of $300,000. Because of the moderate amount of capital involved and the fact that there is little or no income from other sources, such a person may make a policy decision that up to 30 per cent could be exposed to stock market risk (including the risk of a decline of 40 per cent or more in a cyclical slump with up to ten years to recovery). The policy would be that the amount invested in stocks should vary between zero and $90,000. In constructing a portfolio, in terms of the number of stocks and average amount invested, the steps would be as under:

Maximum amount for stock investment according to policy range 30% of $300,000 $90,000

Timing and strategy decision — if stock prices are well above the long term trend and other indicators discussed elsewhere are unfavourable, limit stock investment to 25 per cent of capital of $300,000, which means an amount of $75,000

Reserve for special situations — allow 15 per cent of this amount for special situations such as those discussed above, which is an amount of about $11,000

This leaves an amount for current investment of   **$64,000**

Number of stocks in portfolio — a suitable figure would be   8

So average amount per stock would be $64,000 divided by 8, which equals $8,000

Maximum amount per stock, except in very unusual circumstances, would be average amount multiplied by 2, equals $16,000

Minimum amount per stock would be average amount divided by 2, which equals $4,000

When to review portfolios

Portfolios should be under more or less constant review, but a more detailed overall review of the portfolio is necessary in the following circumstances:

➤ **Regular periods** — Perhaps every three months or six months would be an appropriate time.

➤ **Change in market conditions** — If, over a period of even a month or two, there is a very large change in prices — e.g. the frantic rise at the end of the boom in 1987 — a special review of the situation may be necessary to consider whether precautionary selling is needed. This would ensure that the gains that have been made are not eroded by any subsequent slump and that you have cash available for purchase of stocks at favourable prices after the slump.

➤ **Change in investor's conditions** — A change in an investor's conditions, such as approaching retirement, an increase or decrease in family responsibilities, an increase or decrease in income from a profession, salary or business. Potential changes in those factors or possible threat to employment would all be matters which could warrant a special review of your portfolio, including your portfolio policy in some cases.

➤ **Changes in the law** — Changes in the law, or in company tax rates, are other factors which could necessitate a portfolio review.

How to review portfolios

In reviewing portfolios the following principles should be followed:

1. **Consider the present and the future** — Consider present yield, present price relative to the rest of the market, present situation of the overall stock market in relation to average dividend yield, long term trend and estimates of future dividends and earnings of the company and prospects for the economy.

2. **Use current prices and yields** — In considering whether to sell a stock it is the *current* yield, based on *current* price, which is relevant. That yield may be much lower than the yield an investor is deriving on his cost price of many years ago, but it is the *current* situation which must be considered.

3. **Do not "fall in love" with your stocks** — Many people make the mistake of holding stocks because they have a high

regard for the directors and management or because the stock has done very well for them in the past. This is not a sound approach to a review of a portfolio. In investments, there is no truth in the old saying that if you are on a good thing stick to it. Very often the good thing you are on may well be the stock which you should sell because of the probability that high rates of gain in the past may not be maintained and could be followed by a significant reduction in stock prices. Even if earnings are maintained, prices could decline, simply as a reaction to excessive enthusiasm of the past.

4. **Opportunity cost** — Remember even if you have to sell at a loss it may be wise to do so rather than to hold stocks indefinitely in the hope that they may eventually recover to your cost price. Opportunity cost of the income and possible capital gain prospects foregone by a long wait for recovery can make it very costly.

5. **The step system** — Remember that in buying and selling, particularly in selling, you should use the step system. If you feel there is a case for selling but are hesitant to sell all of a holding or all of your stocks, because the market may continue to rise, then consider selling first a portion — perhaps a third or a quarter — and then watching the market closely for the timing of any further sales.

Chapter 9

Selecting Stocks
to Buy

"When I use words they mean what I want them to mean".
That quotation from *Alice in Wonderland* would be a good
description of many terms used in the share market and
investment industry.

In any other business, a group of stocks which over many
years had failed to do as well as the average and in bad times
had performed worse than the average would probably be
called disappointing. But in the stock market, many of those
stocks are called leaders or "blue chips".

So the first lesson in considering how to select stocks for a
portfolio is to avoid the widely publicised fallacies of the
importance of investing in leaders or blue chips or quality
stocks. Some of those stocks, some of the time, perform
extremely well. But they are not the assured path to success or
the safe haven in troublesome times which the conventional
wisdom suggests.

Essentials of stock selection

Below the essentials in selection of stocks are summarised:

◆ *Timing*

Sometimes the best stock to buy may be none at all. The time
of buying stocks, and more particularly the time of selling
them, often has a far more important effect on investments
than what stocks you buy. So it is important to remember that
highly regarded stocks may not turn out to be a good
investment if they are bought at the wrong time or at an
unrealistic price which is unlikely to be maintained in the
medium to long term.

◆ *Overall importance of price*

Shares in a company which is in a sound financial position with a good earnings and dividend record and good prospects for the future, may be a very good buy at a price of say $2.00. At some time later, when it is strongly being recommended by stockbrokers and financial writers at a price of $5.00, it may no longer be good to buy because of the possibility of subsequent decline. Remember that even if the company maintains and increases its earnings, the share price may decline significantly in value simply as a reaction to the excessive enthusiasm of the past.

◆ *Consider four elements of return*

The four elements of return from investing in shares are:

1. The dividend yield (i.e. the dividend related to the cost price per share)

2. A gradual increase in dividends

3. The dividend tax credit

4. A capital gain or loss due to change in prices.

Generally, it is the fourth component which has the most significant impact on the results of share investments. This underlines the importance of timing and of considering price as well as the record of the stock. Remember that if you buy stocks on a low dividend yield, well below the market average, your "actual money" component is small and you are relying more heavily on this "maybe money" of capital gain.

◆ *Relatively low downside risk*

Serious declines in stock markets, that may take up to ten years to recover, have a tendency to occur when most people in the investment industry are very enthusiastic about stocks. For that reason it is a good plan to select stocks in which the downside risk is somewhat reduced. One good way of achieving this goal is to select stocks which are sound in other respects and also offer a dividend yield above the market average. In the event of a decline in the market, the gradually increasing return, as the result of that decline in price, should attract buying support which should limit the decline.

By contrast, stocks bought at high points in the market on a dividend yield of 2 per cent or so may continue to slide by 50 per cent or more. Even after that reduction, their yield in the more sober assessment of a slump may be unattractive.

Some of these factors are discussed in more detail below.

Why relative price is so important

When we are talking of price, obviously it is a matter of *relative* price. The fact that one stock is selling at $3.00 and another at $1.00 does not necessarily mean that the former stock is more expensive. If it is providing a higher dividend yield with a lower price earnings multiple, and has equal or better prospects than the latter stock, then it may be more attractively priced. In this discussion on price we are thinking in terms of price compared with other stocks in terms of dividend yield, price earnings multiple and the other factors (which will be discussed further in Chapter Seventeen), with due allowance for an estimate of future prospects.

Many recommendations for purchase of stocks, or purchase of unit trusts which invest in stocks, almost completely ignore price. The recommendations are based entirely on factors such as the record of the company to date, the quality of its management and its future prospects. All those matters are important up to a point. But it is not sound to buy a stock simply because it is highly recommended if its price, relative to other shares, is very high. It is not sound practice to buy simply on other qualities of the stock that may not be nearly strong enough to justify its price, producing a yield half or less than half of the market average.

A good deal of research by stockbrokers and institutions into the earnings and prospects for companies is of a high quality. But where it falls down is that this sort of research seems to work on the assumption that the purpose of the research is to more or less award a "housekeeper's seal of approval" on such a stock and to reward it by a buying recommendation. It tends to overlook the fact that, even if all those other attractive qualities are there, the stock may not be a good buy because previous enthusiasm and previous recommendations of that type have pushed the price up to an unrealistic level.

To put it another way, investors often make more profit out of buying stocks with a moderate record and moderate prospects — at a reasonable price — rather than buying stocks with a very good record and prospects — at an excessive price — relative to other stocks.

Market happenings can be more important than company results

Another weakness of most of the discussion and recommendation of stocks is that it overlooks one vital fact. That fact is that often what happens in the market, including overall cyclical movements, the mood of the moment being one of either reckless enthusiasm or deep gloom, and changes in what is flavour of the month with local and international investors, often has a far larger bearing on the success of an investment than the results, financial position or prospects of the company.

The impact of psychological factors on the market is discussed in Chapter Eighteen.

The point has already been made that the so-called blue chips, the quality stocks, the leaders, in general have not performed as well as other less prestigious stocks. Moreover, the downside risk of these stocks is greater because their decline in cyclical slumps is often more severe and prolonged.

Comments on various types of stocks

Brief comments on various categories of stocks follow:

♦ *Second ranking stocks — tomorrow's leaders.*

For reasons discussed above, stocks other than leaders have generally been the better performers over the last 30 or 40 years. To put it another way, you can generally do a lot better, not by investing in today's leaders but in tomorrow's leaders — the second ranking, middle of the range stocks which may achieve "leader" status and higher market ratings which will accentuate the gains that may be achieved while generally offering a lower downside risk than the leaders.

◆ *Speculative stocks*

In conventional investment industry thinking, speculative stocks are those stocks which are considered to have a very high risk. They include the stocks with a high intrinsic risk, such as mineral exploration stocks and companies going into new ventures with no performance record. In fact, like many other investment terms, the term "speculative" is somewhat misleading because when you analyse it, all investments in the stock market involve speculation. Whether you are buying stocks in Johnny-Come-Lately Mining NL or a " blue chip", you are speculating or backing your judgement that, for whatever reason, the market will pay a higher price for these stocks in the future than the price at which you are buying them.

◆ *Glamour stocks*

At various times in the market, stocks become glamour stocks. At some times high technology stocks may be top of the speculators' hit parade, at others it may be conglomerates.

◆ *Possible takeovers*

Stocks which seem to offer prospects of being taken over may produce very good results for investors. But be wary of those stocks where widespread rumours of possible takeovers have already pushed up their price to levels from which a severe decline could occur if the takeover does not eventuate. Try to select stocks which may offer takeover prospects but are still reasonably priced relative to the rest of the market, so that if the takeover offer does not eventuate there will not be a great decline in price.

Perhaps all of these points could be summed up in the statement that there is really no such thing as a "good stock". There may be good companies but, if the whole market or the price of that particular stock is at unrealistically high levels, then that "good" stock may produce serious losses rather than gains.

Superficial analysis of stocks is not sufficient

Much of the traditional analysis of stocks is superficial. This is probably one reason why so many institutions suffer significant losses in stocks which produce disappointing results. This matter is discussed in more detail in Chapter Seventeen.

Some basic financial indicators

Some basic indicators which are a guide to the relative value of stocks are set out below:

➤ **Price dividend multiple (p.d.)** — This is price per share divided by dividend yield. It is the reciprocal of the dividend yield.

➤ **Dividend yield** — Dividend per share divided by price per share and multiplied by 100 to express as a percentage.

➤ **Price earnings multiple (p.e.)** — Price per share divided by earnings per share.

➤ **Dividend cover** — This is earnings per share divided by dividend per share. It is generally wise to invest in stocks with ample cover so that even after there is a significant decline in earnings per share, the dividend rate and hence the yield should be maintained. Generally a cover of more than 1.25 is desirable.

➤ **Return on equity** — This is the earnings after tax and any preference share dividend as a percentage of net equity. A decline in this rate, even if earnings per share are increasing, could indicate a possible future decline or slowing down of the rate of growth. Most of the stocks which appeal to the discerning investor generally have been on an earnings on net equity rate of 12 per cent or more.

(See Chapter Seventeen for description of more refined indicators.)

Share trading and stocks for a flutter

The above comments about selection of stocks are primarily for the average investor who does not have the capital, and who is not in a position, to engage in share *trading* involving purchase and sale of shares in the short term, sometimes a matter of days or weeks. To engage successfully in that type of operation involves being able to afford much larger risk and time to watch share prices, not only by the day but sometimes by the hour. It also calls for steady nerves and the ability to make unpleasant decisions to cut losses rather than to run the risk of greater losses when the market does not co-operate with the trader's hopes.

Share trading calls for a greater concentration on short term market behaviour. In the short term, there is the effect of changes in what is flavour of the month, in the herd-like instinct of large investors and institutions and in the volatile behaviour of international investors. Share traders seek to sense the situation where a quick rise, either in the overall market or in a particular section of it, may be likely.

Successful share traders decide to let their profits run and to cut their losses by very close study of what is happening in the market as distinct from what they or anybody else feels should happen in the market. In making any additional investments in a stock the wise trader makes the second investment a smaller amount than the first, and the third smaller than the second, and so on. That means that in the event of a sudden turn in the market the loss is reduced because a smaller portion of the total investment has been acquired at the very high price prior to the decline. Some traders also make use of options and futures trading which are discussed in Chapter Nineteen.

Sometimes investors, who are not traders and who wish to keep their risk to the minimum, may decide to set apart a **small portion** of their capital, perhaps 5 per cent to 10 per cent, to use in trading. It is essential that they limit the amount, so that if the market does not co-operate with their predictions the loss would not be great. This activity is certainly not one in which you would wish to invest next week's housekeeping money or funds that you have put aside for the education of the children or for other purposes.

Chapter 10

Stock Prices
Relative to Long
Term Trend

Tourists in Ireland, frustrated by the inability of a farm labourer to tell them which was the road to Killarney, made some scathing comments about the ignorance of Irish country people. To this the farm labourer replied, "at least I know where I am". "Then why can't you tell us which is the road to Killarney", said the tourists. "Because", the labourer replied, "if I were going to Killarney I certainly wouldn't be starting from here".

The best results in share investing are generally achieved by those who know just where the market is at any particular time — just where it is in relation to its long term trend.

What is the long term trend?

A trend generally indicates a general direction. In statistics, it is used to indicate the general direction of various indicators as distinct from the ebb and flow of the monthly or quarterly statistics. Trends are useful in helping to separate out the general direction of sets of figures as distinct from short term movements which may be of only temporary significance.

In the stock market, the long term trend is a figure calculated by a statistical method known as the "least squares" method. In lay persons terms, in a somewhat simplified way, it could be described as the general direction of share prices over a long period.

It could also be seen as the rate of gain which the share market is likely to maintain in the long term, as distinct from the very high rate of rise in prices in booms and significant decline in slumps.

The long term trend in share prices is an upward movement at the rate of about 6.5 per cent per annum. This result is based on least squares calculations over a period of about 30 years.

An extremely interesting point is that if trends are calculated for periods of more than 15 or 20 years the trend figure does not vary a great deal from the figure of 6.5 per cent per annum. In other words, the excesses of one medium to long term period tend to be offset by significantly different movements in the previous or succeeding period.

For example, during the 10 years from July 1982 to July 1992 share prices rose at a very high rate of 12.2 per cent per annum compound. But in the previous 10 years, from July 1972 to July 1982 there was a rise of only 1.7 per cent per annum compound. Taking the two periods together, the 20 year result of 6.8 per cent per annum is fairly close to the long term trend of 6.5 per cent per annum compound. Incidentally, in trend figures it is compound rates that are important, because what we are looking at is the *rate* of change, not the *amount* of change. So an increase from 500 to 550 reflects the same rate of growth as an increase from 1000 to 1100, because each is an increase of 10 per cent.

Long term trend as an indicator of where the market is

Though other indicators which are discussed elsewhere in this book need to be considered, the position of the market relative to its long term trend is a very useful indicator of where the market is. As the figures later in this chapter show, that can also be a good indication of future prospects and downside risk.

As the trend line can be seen as the average direction of the market, comparing the current position of the index with the trend enables us to describe prices as low, average, or high. Because there is an inverse relationship between prices at time of investment and results achieved, it is also possible to describe prospects for the future as favourable, average or unfavourable.

We could set out the relationship this way with *low* being the situation when prices are below the long term trend and *high* when it is above.

Prices	How Favourable to Investors?	Prospects of Good Results	Downside Risk of Loss
Very low	Most	Very good	Very Low
Fairly low	Moderately	Fairly good	Low
Average	Average	Average	Average
High	Unfavourable	Poor	High
Very high	Very Unfavourable	Very poor	Very high

The above relationship may not necessarily apply in the short term. In the later stages of a boom, buying at high prices may lead to very good short term results but only to the fleet of foot traders who are smart enough to get out before the boom turns into a slump. Buying at low prices may be followed for a time by a continued decline in prices until the recovery gets under way. But as the law of gravity has not been repealed, logic would suggest that the above relationship would be true in the medium to longer term. It is confirmed by my research figures which are discussed below.

Range of variation above and below trend

The extent of variations above and below the long term trend, which is also an indication of the longer term volatility of the stock market, can be seen from looking at the figures below for the extreme high and low points in the 35 years up to December 1994.

High point September 1987 139.8% **above long term trend**

Low point September 1974 56.75% **below long term trend**

The first point to note is that in January 1994 when so many investment people were confidently predicting that, even after the rises in 1993 the market would continue to rise to much higher levels, they were ignoring the following lessons of history:

1. The market at that time was 66 per cent above the long term trend, well into the very high price Zone 1 which is the most unfavourable zone for investing.

2. With the exception of nine months in 1987, that was the highest the market had been relative to long term trend for about 50 years.

3. The record showed that in the past, the medium term — five years — results from investing in the share market when it was more than 35 per cent above long term trend, had been very disappointing. Investing in those conditions produced an average five year **capital loss** of 1.1 per cent per annum compound. Five year capital gain of more than 5.0 per cent per annum compound was achieved in only one fourteenth of the total number of periods. The maximum five year gain achieved was 7.0 per cent — just a little above the worst result achieved from investing when prices were very low, i.e. at Zone 5.

4. Under those circumstances, the downside risk was much greater with the worst five year period showing a loss of 57 per cent of capital. So on both prospects of capital gain and downside risk of loss, the very high share prices in January 1994 were clearly in the most unfavourable Zone, i.e. Zone 1 in the zone ranking system described below.

◆ *Dividend yield also very ominous*

If the alternative approach of considering share prices on the basis of average dividend yield had been used, the figures would have been similarly ominous. The average dividend yield at the peak of the market, early in February 1994, was 2.7 per cent. On that basis share prices were at an all time peak except for a couple of months in 1987. They were well and truly into Zone 1 which is the most unfavourable — see comments in Chapter One.

Investment results from investing at high or low prices

My research into the relationship between the position of the stock market related to long term trend and medium term results produced interesting figures.

♦ *Rating scale using zones*

For the research, medium term results for five year periods were studied. The study was of capital gain after allowing for estimated buying and selling brokerage of 1.5 per cent. The study concentrated on capital gain or loss because that component of overall return is generally the most significant. It is high capital gain which is the main contributor to excellent results in stock market investments and serious capital losses which are the main contributor to poor results.

Moreover, the contrast between good results from investing when prices are below the long term trend would be accentuated if income were considered. Periods when prices are below the trend are generally periods when initial dividend yield and probable rate of increase in dividend increases are high and vice versa.

The research covered 360 rolling periods each of five years starting with the period from January 1960 to January 1965 and ending with the period from December 1989 to December 1994. The periods were classified into five zones of varying percentages — above or below the long term trend — with approximately equal numbers of periods. The zones are an indication as to whether prices are low or high and hence favourable or unfavourable to investors (see table below).

Zone	Price	Range of Prices Related to Trend
5	Very low	-56.8% to -25.01%
4	Low	-25.0 % to -1.01%
3	Average	-1.00% to +8.25%
2	High	+8.26% to +34.99%
1	Very high	+35% to +139.79%

Logic and common sense would suggest an inverse relationship, with high prices related to trend at time of investing, producing poor results with greater downside risk of losses and vice versa. This is how the figures came up in terms of capital gain or loss per cent per annum compound.

Zone	Range of 5 year capital gain or loss		
	Average	Minimum	Maximum
5	15.0%	6.1%	33.4%
4	10.4%	loss of 3.4%	27.7%
3	4.4%	loss of 7.9%	15.3%
2	2.3%	loss of 15.5%	11.0%
1	loss of 1.1%	loss of 15.5%	7.0%

Many aspects of the figures are worth noting. The average gain from investing when prices are very low, i.e in Zone 5 is more than **six times** the gain in the high price Zone 2 — a marked contrast to the loss of 1.1 per cent in very high price Zone 1.

As for downside risk, the worst result from investing in Zone 5, the very low price zone, the minimum result achieved was 6.1 per cent With that amount of capital gain, plus the relatively high income that would have been available in those conditions, it could be said that downside risk is slight as the worst result is still pretty good.

Contrast that with investing in the very high price zone which is Zone 1, where the worst result was **a loss of 15.47 per cent per annum compound. That works out at total loss of 57 per cent over five years.**

Any warning of the possibility of such a serious loss resulting from investing in January 1994, was as scarce as the proverbial hen's teeth in the enthusiastic comments of the conventional investment wisdom at that time about future price rises.

♦ *Significance of above figures*

Those figures are extremely significant. They show quite clearly that there is a strong case for reducing share market involvement when prices move into the very high price Zone 1, and to a lesser extent the high price Zone 2. Similarly, the excellent results with little downside risk from investing when the index is in the very low price Zone 5 and to a lesser extent in the low price Zone 4 suggests that those are the conditions when it would be wise to consider increased share investing, within the maximum set down for policy reasons.

◆ *Prices related to trend and dividend yield*

The findings in this study of the relationship between share prices and long term trend are broadly similar to the results from investing in Zone 5 compared with Zone 1 on the basis of price dividend multiple (see discussion in Chapter One).

Both sets of figures show that there are far more realistic ways of deciding on whether to increase or reduce investment in shares than the widely popular, but seriously misleading, comments of the conventional investment wisdom such as the following:

➤ Timing does not matter

➤ It is always a good time to buy shares

➤ Prices will rise because company earnings are likely to rise, or because interest rates may decline, or overseas investors are being attracted to Australian stocks (at times when the beneficial effects of such factors have already been over-anticipated by the market in rises of 50 per cent or more in the last years or so.)

An objective approach

This type of approach, together with the zone ranking method in relation to average dividend yield, is the most realistic which has emerged during my 40 year experience of the investment business. The great merit of this approach is that it is objective and it is based on what has actually happened in the market over many years. Though that does not make it infallible, it is conceptually sounder than other approaches including the efficient market hypothesis and the capital asset pricing model to which reference was made in Chapter One.

Chapter 11

Market Cycles
and Normal
Trading Range

My mind is made up, don't try to confuse me with the facts.
That attitude, which may affect many of us at various times, is
nowhere more evident than in the investment business in
relation to market cycles and share, or in property for that
matter. To ignore cycles, to pretend that they do not exist, or
to brush them off as being of no importance is to ignore the
lessons of history.

Human behaviour in various fields changes from time to
time. If that were not so the Beatles would still be on top of the
Hit Parade, women would be wearing fashions of the
"thoroughly modern Millie" flapper era of the 1920s and male
business executives would still be viewing the business scene
over winged collars.

A zig zag path

The course of share prices is rather like the way in which very
intoxicated people move from point A to point B. They know
where they want to go, but drift first to one side, then to the
other side, and so on. Or it is rather like the pattern which
even the most abstemious people tend to experience when they
are first learning to drive a car or a boat — moving too much
to one side, then overcorrecting and swinging too much to the
other side.

The track from A to B which the market is likely to
maintain, is the long term trend which was discussed in the
previous chapter. The zig zagging pattern that varies from the
path makes up the cyclical path of the market. In the share

market, the extent of the cycles is greatly magnified for the reason referred to earlier in the text — namely, that so many people in the investment business make a lot of money out of concealing risk and failing to point out to investors how cyclical movements can greatly affect their investments.

Remember the statement by George Soros which was quoted in Chapter One, that the more people believe the efficient market hypothesis, the more unstable markets become.

The reality of large swings and the myth of steady rises

According to the conventional investment wisdom, for stocks, and indeed property, an upward rising trend is a preordained state of affairs. Any departure from that upward trend is seen as a temporary mental aberration. According to that view, after a slight decline the market will regain its senses and return to its preordained path. To put it another way, God's in his heaven, the All Ordinaries is rising and all is well with the world.

One side-effect of this conventional wisdom is the widely publicised belief that if you buy only good quality stocks, or so called blue chips or leaders, you will in some magical way be protected from major swings in prices. But the reality is different. The upward trend of about 6.5 per cent per annum in stock prices is not achieved through anything like a steady movement.

There are wide swings both above and below the long term trend. That is the reality within which share investment decisions must be made. Those who recognise that reality and take it into account in their investment decisions, will do far better than those who accept the conventional wisdom and ignore the reality of market cycles.

What investors have to realise are two very important points:

➣ The long term upward trend is moderate — a rise of about 6.5 per cent per annum compound.

➣ Cyclical swings above and below the long term trend are very great.

The difference from the top of a peak to the trough of a slump, has been as much as 70 per cent for leaders and 45 per cent for other stocks. The rise from the low point, or trough of a slump, to the high point before the next slump commences can sometimes represent a gain of more than 300 per cent.

The relationship of those two figures is very significant. If the long term upward trend were greater or if the extent of cyclical swings were much smaller, it would not matter so much. But it is obvious that if you move into the market just before a cyclical slump, the decline of up to 60 per cent or more is going to leave you behind for a very long time. It may be ten years or more in extreme cases, before the moderate upturn trend puts you in a situation where you are ahead.

Periods of cycles

♦ *Variable periods*

When I warned, in 1987, that a slump could be near and that it could be severe, one of the factors leading to that conclusion was the fact that there had been no cyclical slump for about six years. (The other factors were that both in relation to price dividend multiple and to the long term trend, share prices had been in the very high zone, indeed at record heights, for some time.)

In mid 1987, the period of well over six years from the previous major peak in November 1980 was significant because the length of a cycle from peak to peak had generally been in the range of about two years to four years. But there is considerable variation in the lengths of cycles. So it is not possible to set your alarm clock, so to speak, and expect a boom to end and a slump to start after any specific period.

Major cycles and minor cycles

Sometimes there are minor cycles, or what may be called sub-cycles, within longer cycles. These are movements involving a decline from a peak and then a recovery within a matter of months or a year or so. They can be most realistically viewed as a temporary interruption of the prevailing longer term movement.

In a sense they are a somewhat lengthened version of the ebb and flow of market movements above or below the general direction in which the market is heading. An example was the decline at the end of 1983 and a recovery which had taken the market back up to its earlier level before the end of 1984. Another was the minor cycle to the peak in the All Ordinaries Index in September 1989 at 1789, which was a partial recovery from the slump which started in September 1987 when the peak was 2306.

As the long term average price movement is an upward trend of about 6.5 per cent per annum, a major cycle could be expected to reach a peak higher than the peak of the last major cycle. On that basis, the peak of 1789 in September 1989 which was 22 per cent below the September 1987 peak would clearly be classed as the end of a minor cycle.

The peak of 2341 on the All Ordinaries early in February 1994 raises an interesting question. That peak was 1.5 per cent higher than the September 1987 peak which was passed just a few days earlier. So on the above basis it would qualify as the peak of a major cycle.

But there are two unusual features. One is the small margin by which that peak exceeded the 1987 peak. The other was the fact that within a week of passing the 1987 peak the market had dropped below it again. A year later, in February 1995, the index was 20 per cent below the 1987 peak and 21 per cent below the February 1994 peak. So from a practical point of view, the February 1994 peak seems to be more in the nature of the peak of a minor cycle.

◆ *Growing instability*

The fact is that the duration of cycles was more variable when there was an explosive growth in the number of people promoting share-based investments. These people were usually also in the business of risk concealing and *Goebbeling*. It was also the period in which the efficient market hypothesis was very influential.

Normal trading range

◆ *Description of normal trading range*

Allied to the consideration of market cycles and long term trend is the concept of normal trading range for various markets, which I developed about 20 years ago. It is a recognition of the fact that stock markets, as well as commodity and other markets, tend to have the following features:

➤ A long term trend, generally upward at a moderate rate.

➤ Fairly wide swings above and below that trend.

➤ For most of the time about two thirds of the total trading occurs in an area bounded by the lines about 25 per cent to 35 per cent above and below the trend line. That area is the normal trading range.

A more precise estimate of the levels of the upper and lower limits is discussed below.

◆ *Analogy to quality control charts*

Though a good deal less precise and less scientific, the normal trading range approach can be compared with quality control charts which are used in industry. These charts comprise the average performance measured against a relevant standard.

Upper and lower limits are plotted on the chart, generally three standard deviations above and below the average. The standard deviation is a measure of dispersion from the average or mean. Regular samples are taken from a process and the results plotted on this chart. So long as they fall within the upper and lower limits on that chart the process is said to be in control. If a sample falls outside those limits, it is considered to be out of control. In that event, steps are taken to try to ascertain the reason for the variation and to remedy it.

Normal trading range in the share market

◆ *Use in the share market*

When share market prices are in the area either above the upper boundary or below the lower boundary trading range, they are in what could be called "action areas" — by way of analogy to the out of control areas in the quality control charts.

Naturally the action called for would be to reduce stock market investments when prices are above the upper limit. When they are below the lower limit increased investment in stocks would be the appropriate action.

This does not mean that stocks should be sold with gay abandon in the former case or bought with reckless enthusiasm in the latter. Action to increase or reduce stock market investment should be taken after considering these other relevant factors:

➤ The zone system of ranking stock prices in relation to price dividend multiples or dividend yields, as discussed in Chapter One, and in relation to the long term trend in Chapter Ten.

➤ An assessment of trends for the economy, for the corporate sector, the industry and the particular companies — with proper allowance for the extent to which those factors may already be reflected in stock prices as the result of rises due to market anticipation or, in many cases over-anticipation.

➤ The present portfolio situation in relation to a suitable policy for each individual investor.

➤ The intelligent use of the step system of gradual buying or selling which was discussed in earlier chapters.

➤ The need to take into the account the psychological factors, mob psychology the herd instincts, fads and fashions and market moods of the moment which are discussed in Chapter Eighteen. While buying enthusiasm continues it may be wise to let your profits run on at least some of your holdings with the idea of selling when the market gives some indication that it is running out of steam.

The previous point is particularly important. Seldom, if ever, do markets go into a significant decline without giving some prior indication of weakness. For example, the crash of 1987 is sometimes seen as a rising market suddenly dropping by 20 per cent. The reality is that the market had peaked several weeks earlier and before the big one-day decline it had fallen by about 7 per cent.

◆ *Range above and below the trend*

A comparison of month end figures for the All Ordinaries Index for the period from January 1960 compared with the trend figure reveals the following:

1. For one sixth of the total number of periods the index was above the trend line by 38.6 per cent or more.

2. For one sixth of the total number of periods the index was 28.2 per cent or more below the long term trend line.

3. For two thirds of the total number of periods the index was somewhere between 38.6 per cent above and 28.2 per cent below the trend line. So that area is the estimated normal trading range.

◆ *Example of normal trading range*

The copy of page 3 of the February 1995 issue of *Donnelly's Investing Today* which is included as an Annex to Appendix A gives a chart showing the long term trend, as well as upper and lower limits of the normal trading range for the All Ordinaries Index.

How the normal trading range has been useful

On the principle that one picture is as good as a thousand words, a chart of the normal trading range gives a good first impression of whether share prices are very high, high, average, low or very low. So some impression of the situation can be obtained even before looking more closely at the price zone in relation to long term trend which was discussed in Chapter Ten or in relation to price dividend multiple which was discussed in Chapter One.

It is also particularly helpful in keeping investors' feet on the ground when prices have declined after a boom and the conventional wisdom is confidently predicting that prices must be in the bargain basement. In 1980, when the price of gold had declined from $US850 to about $US600 there were many commentators suggesting that in a few years the price would reach $US3000. The normal trading range showed that it was more likely to be in the $US350 to $US450 range.

It was also useful in a somewhat similar situation in relation to the Australian mineral stocks in the early seventies after they declined from the peak of the Poseidon induced boom of 1969.

◆ *Song of a shirt*

Remember the reference in Chapter Four to the Melbourne investment specialist who stated at the beginning of 1970 that the mineral stocks were so good you could put your shirt on them. If he had used the normal trading range technique, he would not have been without his shirt for most of the last 24 Melbourne winters.

Chapter 12

The Crucial
Importance
of Selling

Within a few days of commencing work in stockbroking in 1955, I heard these sayings:

➤ Nobody ever went broke taking a profit; and

➤ A profit is not a profit until it is in the bank.

Remembering those sayings has helped many investors make wise decisions. Ignoring them has been very costly for many investors.

Arising out of those sayings is a third principle, namely that **eager sellers make good investors**. If you plan to invest in shares (or in property) you must train yourself to be able to face up to selling decisions, even in difficult conditions, for example, when it may mean taking a loss.

The conventional wisdom and selling

It is necessary to over-emphasise the importance of timing and selling simply because it is a subject which tends to be ignored by the conventional investment wisdom. So many comments made by stockbrokers, investment advisers, fund managers and others imply that timing is not important.

Indeed, this is sometimes summed up in the completely false statement that it is not timing that is important, but the time that you are in the market. This is another way of saying that any time is a good time to buy shares. If shares have increased in price, that rise is used to persuade people to buy shares. If shares have declined in price, but only a little, from a very high peak, the argument is that it is again a good time to buy.

Yet a study of the past could show that soon after a slump has commenced, when stocks may be down 10 per cent or so, it is often better business to sell rather than to buy at that stage. The reason is that a slump may take prices down by 40 per cent to 50 per cent and it may be many years before there is a sustained recovery.

Certainly, the suggestion that timing and selling are not important makes life a lot easier for people who are trying to make profits from promoting share investing, directly or through unit trust investing, rather than really analysing the reality of the share market. In fact, every investor who goes into shares should have the following statements prominently displayed on their desk:

➤ **When** you buy, and even more importantly when you sell, is often more important than **what** you buy.

➤ **Never** refrain from selling when analysis suggests that this is the prudent course.

Examples of timing in the short term

In October 1987, the share market declined by about 20 per cent in one day. Two years later, after a partial recovery, a number of stock markets around the world declined about 8 per cent in one day.

Back in 1974, the market declined by about 50 per cent in six or seven months. For those who invested in shares through unit trusts the capital costs of getting into and out of the investment would make the decline worse.

Between September 1986 and 1987 share prices increased by about 50 per cent.

How significant are short term changes?

Some would argue that the sharp up and down movements in prices are generally not significant to most investors, only to active short term traders. Those sharp movements are generally followed in time by reversals which means that their effect tends to be cancelled in the medium to longer term.

That argument is associated with the common, but false claim, that provided you stay in the market for three years or so all will be well.

It is true that for most investors, short term movements in share prices are less significant than movements in the medium or long term. More attention should be given to medium term price movement.

Serious investors should not completely disregard sharp short term movements, for the following reasons:

➢ The extent of a short term rise or fall may be significant as an indication of a possible medium term change. For example, the sharpness of the 1986/1987 rise was one of the factors which suggested that a serious slump was imminent. The severity of the 1974 decline preceded the rise of about 150 per cent over the next six years.

➢ A sharp short term rise or fall can completely change the prospects for capital gain and risk of capital decline. For example, at a certain level when the average dividend yield is 6 per cent, share market investing is attractive (it would be in Zone 5 on the zone ranking system outlined in this book). A quick market rise of 100 per cent makes a great difference. The yield would then be about 3 per cent (perhaps a little more if dividend rates increased much in that short period). At that stage the market is in Zone 1 which, on the basis of previous experience, makes it far from attractive.

The significance of medium term timing

In Chapter One and in other parts of the book there are references to the difference between the capital gain achieved by investing at different times. Over the last 12 years, the classic example has been the difference between the great results from investing in 1982 before the frantic boom and selling in 1987 — compared with investing in September 1987 and selling in September 1992.

So long as there is a situation of a moderate upward trend of about 6.5 per cent per annum in share prices with very wide fluctuations above and below that trend, timing will be important. The realistic investing approach calls for medium term timing to be an essential ingredient to that approach, for the following reasons:

➢ As there is no way to predict the precise time or the precise index level at which turning points will occur, increasing share investments in the lower phase of market cycles and reducing them in the higher phases can make a big difference.

➤ Even moderate success in applying timing principles has produced considerably better results than those achieved by following the timing-does-not-matter approach. Following that approach is really a matter of applying the "jelly fish" philosophy of just drifting up and down with the market tide.

The significance of timing to which reference has been made in other parts of the book can be summarised as under:

Buying investments when the market is attractively priced, i.e. in Zones 4 or 5 on the ranking system described in earlier chapters, produces a significantly higher initial dividend return. That means that compared with investing at other times, the investor is ahead in the important component of the actual money of overall returns as distinct from the maybe money of capital gain.

Initial relatively high income yield generally means that there will be greater scope for share prices to increase (leading to a reduction in later dividend yields), than at times when shares are bought when price dividend multiples are high, i.e. dividend yields are low. Hence, the higher income yield is accompanied by better prospects of good medium to long term capital gain.

As well as providing better prospects of both income and capital gain, applying medium term timing principles to the purchase and sale of investments also greatly reduces the downside risk of capital loss.

Developing a capacity for making selling decisions

Buying decisions are relatively easy. From a study of the shares or from recommendations from a reliable adviser, investors can become very enthusiastic, and placing a buying order presents no mental problem.

But in selling the position is very different. Psychologically it is harder to make selling decisions because to some investors there seem to be many negative aspects to selling decisions. If it is a stock in which they have done very well, they may feel that selling is like turning their back on an old friend. Sometimes, investors hesitate to sell because they have a high regard for the directors and management of the company. But even more than those reasons, many people fail to sell for fear that after they sell the price may rise even further.

Unfortunately, many stockbrokers are not good at suggesting that clients should sell. Some very conscientious brokers fear that a selling recommendation may be seen by their clients as an attempt to earn brokerage by "churning" their portfolio. Others feel that selling recommendations may prejudice their chance to do business as underwriters or brokers for issues by the relevant company.

There is also a feeling among some broking people that to recommend the sale of a share is a form of criticism of the company. It is, in fact, no such thing; it is simply an expression of an opinion that the market has pushed the prices up so far that the investors would be better off by selling all or some of their shares and reinvesting elsewhere.

Some investors more or less persuade themselves not to sell by thinking of excuses such as, if I sell where would I put the money? The answer to that is simple. If there is a sound case for selling, then there is always a place to reinvest the proceeds — sometimes in other shares, sometimes in short term investments to hold the funds temporarily pending a cyclical slump in the market so that funds are available to make a purchase at a better price later on.

Sometimes selling decisions are very hard if they involve selling at a loss. But over and over again experience has shown that when share prices decline, the wisest course may be to sell and take a small loss rather than a much larger loss later on. There is also the question of the opportunity cost to which reference has been made earlier — namely the fact that to hold a stock for many years in the hope of recovery can involve a significant cost in foregoing income and capital gain that could have been earned elsewhere.

In making selling decisions forget your cost price

In making selling decisions it is the present and future with which you are concerned. The price you paid for the share is not really relevant. Whether the sale decision would involve being in the happy position of selling to take a profit or the unhappy position of selling to take a loss, should not affect the decision.

For this purpose it is better, as far as possible, to completely forget the price paid for the shares. One good way of doing this is that, apart from the records which must be kept for accounting or taxation purposes, the records of periodical reviews for your shares should be on current values. As indicated earlier, in looking at the yield on shares, you must consider not the high yield that you may be getting because you bought the shares many years ago at a lower price, but the yield available on the current market and current dividends.

Some circumstances when selling may be wise

The comments above give an indication of the basic considerations of timing in relation to selling decisions. A number of situations in which selling may be warranted are set out below.

1. Because of a change in conditions, whether in relation to the investor's situation, the overall share market situation or the situation of a particular stock, the reasons for initially buying and later for continuing to hold the stock no longer apply.

2. To convert the maybe money of unrealised gain to the actual money of realised gain.

3. As a protection against erosion in an imminent slump of all the gains that have been built up.

4. As similar protection in relation to a particular share which has risen very rapidly in the past.

5. When investors would no longer be prepared to buy that share at the current prices, dividend yield and price earnings multiple, if they did not already hold it.

The last point is a very useful guide as to whether to sell. The idea is to temporarily assume that you are not holding the share, and then ask, on all of the information now available as to future share market prospects, the dividend yield and future prospects of this stock and other factors, would I now wish to buy this stock? If the answer to that question is not a fairly definite yes, then you should start to think seriously about selling it.

Remember the step system

Many prudent investors use the step system to which reference has been made in earlier chapters. Instead of selling the whole of a holding or the whole of their shares, they decide initially to sell a portion of them, perhaps a third or a quarter, as protection against any sudden downturn in market price. Then they watch market movements closely for the timing of any further sales.

The most famous investor and selling

You do not have to take my word for the fact that selling decisions are part of successful investment. The legendary Warren Buffett who is Chairman and Chief Executive Officer of Berkshire Hathaway, in Omaha, Nebraska in the US, is a person generally regarded as by far the most successful investor in the US and probably in the world.

He strongly believes that stocks which meet his high standards (including sound management, continuing earnings growth, satisfactory trend in return on equity, and favourable long term prospects), should be held despite fluctuations in the economy or the share market. But sales are made when warranted. Of the ten stocks in the 1983 Berkshire Hathaway common stock portfolio, only two, GEICO and the Washington Post Company were in the 1993 portfolio.

Chapter 13

Indicators to
Increase or
Decrease Stock
Investments

"Nobody rings a bell at the top or bottom of the market." That old market saying is still very true. It is futile to try to predict the exact market level or date at which a boom turns into a slump or vice versa. But the point has been made in earlier chapters that medium term timing is practicable.

Even moderate success in timing the purchase and sale of investments can considerably increase stock market returns. In addition to achieving a capital gain very much greater than the long term trend of about 6.5 per cent, which would be the average result of the "jelly fish" philosophy of just drifting up and down with the market tide, this procedure generally increases the income. It does that by concentrating on buying at times when yields are more reasonable (as well as when there are better prospects of capital gain) rather than rushing into the market when prices are high and yields are low.

The range of factors that affect share markets

One important point which the conventional investment wisdom fails to make clear is that there are a great number of factors which affect share markets. The conventional investment wisdom more or less suggests that it is a case of "virtue is its own reward". Buy blue chips or quality stocks or leaders and, provided you hold for a long time, results will be very good, says the conventional wisdom. The reality is that share markets are affected by many other factors, other than whether a particular stock is considered as a good stock, a leader, a blue chip or quality stock or a stock you can't go wrong with. The many different factors which affect the share market could be summarised as under:

> **Fundamental factors** — Trends in the local and world economy, interest rates, changes in the corporate share of domestic product and other factors.

> **Market factors** — Such as prices related to the long term trend, cyclical position and relative cost compared with other investments.

> **Psychological factors** — Mob psychology, herd instinct, etc., discussed in Chapter Eighteen.

Fundamental factors

Because listed companies operate in the economy, they are obviously affected by the overall state of the local and world economies. If both the local and world economies are doing well, then, other things being equal, you could expect listed companies to do well and stock prices to improve as a result.

Any change in the corporate sector share of gross domestic product is another factor. Government policy on matters such as tariffs and company tax rates also influence share markets.

Changes in monetary policy can affect companies by making it easier, or more difficult, for them to finance expansion. Changes in interest rates, which are part of monetary policy, can also have an affect for good or ill on company profits. Moreover, other things being equal, changes in interest rates would also be reflected in market prices.

A rise in interest rates would tend to push stock prices down to produce a higher yield to match the higher interest rates available on other investments. The reverse effect would happen when interest rates decline. In practice, that direct effect does not necessarily happen because it may be overwhelmed by other factors, including possible over-anticipation by the share market, or a reaction to earlier over-anticipation. Improvements in productivity or technology can also be favourable.

Market factors

Turning from fundamental factors to market factors, which are so often overlooked by the conventional wisdom, one important item is the position of stock prices as measured by indices such as the All Ordinaries, in relation to the long term market trend.

The cyclical pattern of the market is another. In 1987, when there had been no slump for about six years, that was one of the reasons for indicating that a severe share market slump could be imminent.

The relative cost of stocks compared with the cost of money and interest rates is another. When prices of shares are high as measured by dividend yields compared to interest rates, it is an unfavourable factor for the share market. (Just before the crash in 1987 stock prices had reached such a high level that the interest rates available on medium term investments was almost six times the average dividend yield.)

♦ *Anticipation*

One important factor which is often overlooked is that of over-anticipation. The share market is fairly good at over-anticipating. Indeed, it should be because it spends a good deal of its time doing just that. It has led to two useful market maxims to which reference has already been made:

1. Anticipation is often greater than realisation

2. It often pays to buy on rumour and sell on fact.

A sensible use of indicators

It is essential that the indicators which are discussed below be used sensibly and logically. The decision to move completely, or substantially, into or out of the share market on one indicator would generally not be reasonable. It is necessary to look to more than one indicator before making a decision.

Where some indicators are favourable for the stock market and others are unfavourable, a judgement has to be made as to where the balance lies. If in doubt, it would generally be wise in most cases, to give a greater weighting to the market factors rather than to the fundamentals. The reason is that it is the market factors rather than the fundamentals which have accentuated the force of both booms and slumps.

Indicators for increased stock market investment

The type of indicators which would suggest that investment in the share market could be increased include the following:

➤ Improving local and world economic conditions.

➤ An increase in the corporate share of the gross domestic product.

➤ Improvements in productivity and technology.

➤ Indications that relatively easy money conditions will continue, so that listed companies and the stock market will not be adversely affected by tight money or high interest rates.

➤ The overall stock market position is reasonable in relation to cyclical patterns, the normal trading range and the long term trend. In relation to the last point, the market should be in Zone 5 or 4 of the zone ranking system outlined earlier in the book.

➤ Individual stock prices are attractive on a similar basis.

➤ The relative cost of stocks is low, i.e. that there is not a very large margin between interest rates and dividend yields.

➤ There is not significant evidence that any of the favourable economic indicators shown above have already been over-anticipated by increase in share prices as the result of buying recommendations based on those factors.

➤ On the normal cyclical pattern a cyclical slump does not appear to be due or overdue.

Indicators to reduce share market investment

The indicators suggesting that it is the time to reduce investment in the share market would, in general, be the reverse of the favourable indicators set out above.

Indicators for individual stocks

Naturally, the decisions as to whether to increase or reduce holdings of individual stocks depend to a large extent on the above considerations about the future course of the market. The overall trend of the market is generally, but not always, the most predominant factor in results of a share market investment. But there are some specific factors which are relevant in making decisions on individual stocks. These are discussed in the next few chapters.

Chapter 14

Analysis of Prospects
for the Economy,
the Corporate Sector
and Individual
Companies

There is a story of three university professors who were shipwrecked on a remote island. Also washed up on the shore were containers of food and some explosives. In discussing ways of opening the food container, the professor of engineering said, "It's fortunate for you two that I am here because I can estimate the tensile strength of the containers and so determine the force that is needed to open them without destroying them".

"You would have been in trouble without me", said the professor of chemistry, "because I know the amount of explosives to use to avoid completely destroying the containers and contents".

Whereupon the professor of economics said, "why are we having this discussion at all. Can't we just assume we have a can opener?"

With all due respect to economists, both academic and practicing, a good deal of economic theory is based on a wide range of assumptions, some of which are unrealistic.

Allow for some comment being less than objective

Investors must realise that a good deal of what seems to be authoritative comment on economic matters in the media is less than objective. There are a number of reasons for this situation.

◆ *Group pressures*

The comments on economic matters of highly reputable people in economics and finance may sometimes be a good deal less objective than they would appear, because of the effect of group pressures. Psychological studies show that people in various walks of life have a tendency to make predictions which are not too far away from the consensus. Many specialists hesitate to make predictions which could be seen as "way out". It calls for a fairly high degree of intellectual courage to make predictions which differ significantly from the conventional wisdom. It is well to remember the statement by the late Lord J. M. Keynes quoted earlier, about plaudits tending to go to those who are conventionally unsuccessful, rather than to those who succeed by unconventional means.

◆ *Effect of politics on economic views*

Sometimes comments and predictions in economics and in finance, by specialists in those fields, may be affected to some extent by their political views. In the early eighties, some of the exaggerated claims for supply-side economics and the trickle-down effect of various tax benefits, tended to reflect the conservative political views of many specialists rather than an objective economic analysis.

On the other hand, exaggerated claims by some economists who are politically to the left about the effect of government measures on the economy may also be affected by their political views.

◆ *The human effect*

Comments from what would seem to be authoritative sources on economic matters often lack reliability because they do not give sufficient attention to psychological factors. The reality is that consumers and business people do not always make decisions in the ways in which economists and finance people assume they do.

The effect of anticipation and over-anticipation

The point has been made earlier that good prospects for the whole economy or for an industry or for a particular stock have often been accompanied by *falling* rather than *rising* share prices. The reason is that the good news had been not only anticipated but over-anticipated by the market and a paradoxical decline is the more or less inevitable reaction to that over-anticipation.

To a lesser extent, the same effect can be seen in relation to some comments about trends for the economy. Some commentators may not place sufficient weight on the fact that anticipation of certain changes in trends or fiscal and monetary action by the government or by the Federal Reserve may result in a less than expected effect when they occur.

The local and global economic situation

Listed companies do not operate in a vacuum. They are affected by trends in their industry, their geographical region and in the overall national economy. Stock which may look intrinsically attractive on the basis of its earnings performance, strong financial position and superior management, may be adversely affected by economic factors discussed below. It is necessary to consider possible developments in the industry or in particular regions and in the overall national economy which may have a bearing on the future success of the company and its returns to investors.

Changes in the global economy may also have an effect on stocks. Many stocks will be affected directly because international operations now form a significant part of the business of some Australian companies. Even those companies which are not significantly involved in overseas operations, can be affected. This has become a more important factor in recent years because of fluctuating currency values and integration in international trade and capital movements.

Economic influences — summary

Investors need to realise that their assessment of prospects for particular stocks must be made within the framework of the larger economic factors. So it is important for them to take an active interest in studying published information about the economy. They should then try and interpret that information in the light of the various factors discussed above.

The company

Having looked at the overall economic situation — both locally and globally — and industry trends, we now have to look at prospects for the particular company. To a considerable extent this depends on the ability of the board and management of the company. The companies which tend to do well are those in which the past record and current conditions of the management show an open mind, an ability to be creative and innovative and to grasp new opportunities when they arise. But they do not go overboard in recklessly following the current business fashion.

Sometimes the tone of the annual report and the comments at annual general meetings may be helpful indicators. Companies where the annual report is uninformative and pompous in tone tend to have mediocre management. Evidence of successfully dealing with problems is another matter to consider in assessing companies.

Many analysts in institutions and stockbroking firms place a good deal of emphasis in their findings on visits to the various companies. These may be relevant up to a point. They are probably not as significant as some people would make out. For one thing, the laws relating to insider trading prevent company directors and executives giving significant information in these company visits which is not generally available to shareholders. Moreover, discussions in these company visits may reflect the public relations ability and personality of company executives rather than the real story.

The importance of price

Remember that when you are looking for a company in which to invest, you have to consider the point made earlier about the fact that you are seeking a company which looks attractive and is at a *price* which is reasonable.

Some matters to be considered

The following is a list of some matters which should be considered. Some of them are based on my study and experience but others are based on, or affected by, comments in the book, *The Midas Touch — the Strategies that have made*

Warren Buffett America's Pre-eminent Investor, by John Train, (Harper and Row, New York).

1. Does the company operate in a business where there is reasonable capacity for passing cost increases on to customers?

2. The acid test of the effectiveness within which funds are used (see comments in next chapter).

3. Do comments of the chairman at meetings give an impression of a management which is forward-thinking, innovative and flexible — flexible enough to take advantage of new conditions but stable enough not to make rash investment decisions?

4. As well as reporting good earning figures, does the company also produce a good cash flow? Are total liabilities relatively small in relation to total assets? Do the earnings not rely unduly on gearing benefits from the use of creditors' funds or tax benefits, with the taxation cost being much less than normal? (See further discussion on these subjects in Chapter Seventeen.)

5. Does a thorough study of the notes to the accounts show that earnings figures seem to be reasonably realistic and are not overstated by techniques such as including capital profits as income or debiting certain costs against reserves rather than profit and loss account or any of the other accounting tricks to which reference is made elsewhere in the book?

6. Has the business shown over the years, a reasonable rather than a spectacular rate of growth in net assets? Steady rates of growth are more likely to be sustained than spectacular rates of growth which may last for a few years, but more often than not lead to later financial troubles and perhaps failure.

Chapter 15

Analysis of Individual Stocks — Basic Indicators

This is another area in which I am reminded of the sign, for the guidance of staff, in a war-time store, which read, "Put your trust in God and get a signature from everybody else".

For investors it is important that they make decisions on the basis of an objective analysis of the financial statements of the company. That is not the sole criteria for making investments because psychological factors discussed in Chapter Eighteen are also important.

But you are more likely to succeed in investments if you make decisions on the basis which includes objective analysis, rather than simply buying what are popularly considered to be good stocks. Remember the point made earlier, that there is really no such thing as a good stock, because shares in a good company may turn out to be a poor investment. Price may decline simply as a reaction to excessive enthusiasm in the past and a great amount of buying which was not based on an objective analysis.

Dividend yield and price dividend multiple

➢ **Dividend yield** — is the dividend per share, divided by the price per share and multiplied by 100 to express it as a percentage. If a company is paying a dividend of 12¢ per share and the stock is selling at $3.00, then the yield is 4 per cent. That figure is an indicator of the income return compared to the return available on other investments. Naturally, other factors including a possible increase in dividend receipts over the years and capital gain, and the tax credit on some dividends would also need to be taken into account.

➤ **Price dividend multiple** — Another way of expressing this relationship is the price dividend multiple. It is the price per share divided by dividend per share. On the above figures it is the price of $3.00 divided by dividend of 12¢ which is 25. The price dividend multiple is the reciprocal of the dividend yield.

➤ **Growth in dividend income** — Generally the rate of dividend tends to increase as earnings of companies grow, partly because of income generated by the undistributed earnings which are used in the business.

Growth in dividends

One source of return on shares is the gradual increase in dividends which can be expected over a period of years. Generally, the long term rate of growth in dividends is about 6 per cent. With that rate of growth, a stock purchased on a dividend yield of 4 per cent would be producing an income of about 8 per cent in 12 years (because a growth rate of 6 per cent means a doubling in about 12 years).

But there is a considerable variation in the rate of growth in dividends depending on changing circumstances. In the second half of the eighties, dividend receipts increased greatly. The introduction of the dividend tax credit encouraged many companies to pay out a higher proportion of available profits. Many companies also paid out special dividends to utilise franking credits which had been built up over the years.

Then in the early years of the nineties, dividend receipts declined by up to about 30 per cent for a couple of years. This was partly due to lower earnings, partly to the absence of companies increasing their pay-out ratio because of tight business conditions in the recession, and partly because they no longer had large available franking credits from which to pay tax-free dividends.

This is an important factor for investors to consider. The point has been made earlier in the book, that many investors who thought they were buying shares in Westpac Banking

Corporation in the early nineties, on a very high dividend yield with full tax credit, found later that their dividend receipts were very much lower. Then to add insult to injury, the dividends were not franked and did not attract a tax credit.

Price earnings multiple

The price earnings multiple is the price per share of the company divided by the earnings per share. It differs from the dividend yield in that it is based not on the dividend received by shareholders but on net earnings after tax which is available for distribution to ordinary shareholders. Suppose the company referred to in the above example, which is paying a dividend of 12¢ per share has earnings equivalent to 15¢ per share. Then the price earnings multiple is the price of $3.00 divided by the earnings per share of 15¢ which works out at 20. So that stock has a price earnings multiple of 20.

Earnings

◆ *Earnings per share*

This figure is arrived at by dividing earnings after tax and after any dividend on preference shares by the number of ordinary shares on issue.

◆ *Fully diluted earnings per share*

This figure is the earnings per share after allowing for the extent to which that figure could be diluted after the conversion into ordinary shares on issue by the exercise of options and shares, and the conversion of convertible bonds or preference shares.

◆ *Earnings yield*

Another way of expressing earnings is the concept of earnings yield. In the case of a company earning 15¢ per share, which is priced at $3.00, the earnings yield is 15 divided by $3.00 multiplied by 100 to express it as a percentage, which works out at 5 per cent. This is simply another way of expressing the earnings per share. The earnings yield is the reciprocal of the price earnings multiple, i.e. one divided by the price earnings multiple.

Dividend cover

Dividend cover is the term used to describe the number of times the dividend per share is covered by the earnings per share. In the example above of an earnings yield of 5 per cent (or a price earnings multiple of 20), and a dividend yield of 4 per cent, the dividend cover is 1.25 times, i.e. 5 divided by 4.

In a company in which the dividend is fairly well covered by available earnings, the prospect of a reduction in the dividend, and hence in the yield, is less likely. Such a company could continue to pay the same dividend, even if earnings were to be reduced significantly.

Reviews must be based on current market not cost figures

In reviewing portfolios and deciding whether to continue to hold a particular stock, or to sell all or part of that stock, investors must remember that it is the dividend yield or price earnings multiple based on *current market* which is relevant. Many investors make the mistake of deciding to continue holding a stock because they are getting a very good dividend yield on the cost price of many years ago.

But consideration of the yield or price earnings multiple based on the current market may give a different picture. It may show that the stock is significantly over-priced in relation to the other stocks in the market after considering its prospects. Or, indeed, it may be that the average dividend yield and price earnings multiple for the whole market are so high that a move out of the market could be wise.

This is particularly relevant for older people or retired people or those who do not have income from other sources. By selling a stock which is giving a good dividend yield to them on a much lower cost price of many years ago, and reinvesting the proceeds elsewhere, they may be able to double or treble their income. Alternatively, they could invest all or part of the sum in stocks which may offer greater scope for capital gain in the future.

This is another case of the importance of being on guard against falling in love with your stocks, and remembering the adage, if you would not be keen on buying a particular stock at current dividend yields and price earnings multiple, then you should seriously consider whether you should sell all or part of your holding.

Relative merits of price dividend multiple and price earnings multiple

Many investment analysts are inclined to consider that the use of dividend yield or price dividend multiple is an old-fashioned and unsophisticated approach to investment. They say that it is the price earnings multiple or earnings yield which must be considered. They argue that as shareholders are part-owners of the company, it is the total earnings which are relevant and not only that portion of the earnings which is distributed as dividend. To some extent, that argument is reasonable. But it overlooks one vital point; that is that dividend yield is part of the actual return to investors in shares. The other parts are dividend tax credit, if any, gradual growth in dividend and capital gain or loss.

But the portion of earnings which is not distributed as dividends, is not an actual part of the return on shareholders' funds. The theory is that shareholders will enjoy the benefit of those undistributed earnings in the form of higher stock prices reflecting higher earnings as the result of the use of retained earnings in the expansion of the business.

The reality is different. Whether and to what extent shareholders derive any benefit from earnings which are not distributed, depends on a whole host of market factors. Those factors include changes in the overall mood of the market, the inflow or outflow of overseas capital into the local market, the change of interest rates and the attractions of fixed-interest and other investments.

The point has been made earlier that very often what happens in the market, including a lot of psychological factors, may have a greater influence on the result of an investment than what happens in the company itself. So for that reason there is a case for giving a somewhat greater emphasis to dividend yield. However, it is obvious that the earnings yield or price earnings multiple and the dividend cover are factors which need to be considered.

Relative figures may be more useful

Generally, the most useful figures are relative figures — for example, price dividend or price earnings multiples, relative to the market average, or to the average figure in the past, or related to the cost of money and interest rates available on other investments. (This is discussed further in Chapter Sixteen.)

Market rating of a stock

One of the most useful applications of the principle of the importance of relative figures is the market rating concept which I developed many years ago.

This is stock price dividend multiple divided by market average price dividend multiple. Suppose a stock, paying a dividend of 10¢ is priced at $3.30, i.e a price dividend multiple of 33, (equivalent to a yield of 3.03 per cent). If the average price dividend multiple for the whole market is 22 (equivalent to a yield of 4.55 per cent) the market rating of the stock is 1.5 — 33 divided by 22. Similar calculations could be made on stock price earnings multiple and market average. But for reasons explained earlier, price dividend multiples are generally preferable.

◆ *Dual impact of changes*

If a stock achieves higher than average growth in dividends, or the market reflects higher estimates by analysts of dividends, the value of the stock is likely to increase as the result of the combined effect of two factors:

➤ A higher price to reflect the higher dividend receipts.

➤ Further increase because the increased dividend may result in the stock being awarded a higher market rating.

The higher rating may be due to the stock becoming more popular, or it may be that more institutions discover the attractions of the stock or there are more buying recommendations in brokers' reports and the financial media.

◆ *An example of the dual effect*

The following is an example of how these two forces can affect stock prices. Let us assume first that the dividend receipts increase by 30 per cent, from 10¢ to 13¢, and second, that this is followed by the market pushing prices up to a price where buyers accept a lower yield of 2.27 per cent. In terms of price dividend multiple, which is the reciprocal of dividend yield, that is an increase from 33 to 44. This is how it works out :

◆ *New Value*

A.	Dividend per share	13¢
B.	Price dividend multiple	44
C.	Share price (A multiplied by B)	$5.72

◆ *Old Value*

D.	Dividend per share	10¢
E.	Price dividend multiple	33
F.	Share price (D multiplied by E)	$3.30
G.	Increase in value	$2.42
	Per cent increase (G/F multiplied by 100)	73.3%

If market rating had remained unchanged, the increase in value would have been only 30 per cent to reflect the 30 per cent increase in dividend receipts. It has been increased to 73.3 per cent because the market rating has increased by one third from 1.5 times the market average to twice the market average.

In practice, the effect may differ somewhat from the above figures because of factors such as the extent to which expectations of the increase in dividend had already been reflected in the market price and many other cross-currents. But it is a concept that should not be ignored.

One of the reasons for disappointing results in some stocks which had previously done very well may be seen by an analysis of changing market rating. A good deal of the very good rises in the past may have been due to ever-increasing market rating. Market rating increases cannot continue indefinitely. So there may come a time when increased dividends are accompanied by falling, rather than increasing, prices as the market adjusts the rating from spectacularly high peaks to more sustainable levels.

Using market ratings in investment decisions

Considerations of the effect of changing market ratings should be part of the decision-making process on purchases and sales of shares. Some investors, including some US fund managers have produced a good combination of benefits to risk by using market rating as an aid to selection of stocks and as a means of reducing downside. For example, they may apply the following principles:

➤ In buying stocks, select stocks which are attractive on other criteria and on which the market rating is no higher than about 80 per cent of the market average. For example, if the market average price dividend multiple is 25, (i.e. a yield of 4 per cent) seek stocks with a price divided multiple of no more than 20 (a dividend yield of 5).

➤ As for selling, think about possible partial sales of stocks which are priced at more than about a third or so above the market average. So if the market average price dividend multiple is 25, (i.e. a yield of 4 per cent) consider selling stocks with a price dividend of 33 (a yield of about 3 per cent). But consider other relevant factors including the market mood.

Dividends and overall return on share investments

In *Bogle on Mutual Funds*, Richard D. Irwin Inc. (Burr Ridge Illinois, 1994, P. 11), John Bogle demonstrates the significance of dividend yields in the US markets. Tables show total share return analysed into its three components — initial dividend yield, dividend growth rate, and the impact of multiple change. The later item is the change in price dividend multiple between the beginning and end of the period.

The figures are for decades which John Bogle describes as the golden decade, of 1981 to 1991, the tin decade from 1968 to 1978 and the average decade of all the rolling decades between 1926 and 1992.

The figures are as under :

	1981 to 1991 (%)	1968 to 1978 (%)	Average Decade 1926 to 1992 (%)
Initial dividend yield (p.a.)	+ 5.4	+ 3.0	+ 4.7
Dividend growth rate (p.a.)	+ 6.3	+ 5.1	+ 4.8
Impact of multiple change (p.a.)	+ 6.3	-5.6	+ 1.0
Average annual total return	+ 18.0	+ 2.5	+ 10.5

The total return, in the best decade, of 18.0 per cent per annum was 15.5 per cent above the total return of 2.5 per cent in the worst decade. Of that difference of 15.5 per cent, most of it — 11.9 per cent — was due to difference in the impact of multiple change (+6.3 per cent compared with -5.6 per cent).

Those figures bear out the point made in earlier chapters about investment at low price dividend multiples, i.e. high dividend yields generally offer better prospects of capital gain and a lower probability of capital loss. That is not surprising because, for investments made when dividend yields are fairly high, there is more scope for later market enthusiasm to push prices up and yields down than when they are already at very low levels at time of investment.

◆ *Application to individual stocks*

Though the above figures relate to the overall market, somewhat similar forces apply to individual stocks, especially when market enthusiasm for individual stocks has pushed the price dividend multiple of these stocks relative to other stocks to abnormally high levels, (i.e to relatively low dividend yields).

Importance of trends and estimates of growth

There is an old saying that one swallow does not make a summer. A sharp increase in dividend or earnings per share in one year does not necessarily mean that the improvement will be continued or that the stock is the greatest bargain of the century — unless there is reliable evidence that there has been a radical change in the underlying conditions affecting the company (for example, in a recovery from a previous decline).

Investors should also try to assess the likely future rate of growth in earnings and dividends for some years ahead. As well as the direct effect on investment income from dividends, those growth rates have an effect on the increase or decrease in capital value and possibly a further effect through a change in market rating for the stock.

Public sources of information, such as the growth estimates and research reports of stockbrokers may be helpful. But it is important that investors should be conservative in deciding on what growth estimates to use.

The advice of Benjamin Franklin that a merchant should allow for only one kind of luck, namely, bad luck should be remembered by investors.

Beware of undue reliance on figures

Though it is important to consider the indicators and analysis discussed in this chapter and the next two chapters as thoroughly as possible, remember the results of your investments in shares can be affected by a number of other factors, such as:

➤ Changes in the national and world economies

➤ The cyclical situation of the overall stock market

➤ Changes in the attractions of other investments and interest rates

➤ Mob psychology, the herd instinct, investing fads and fashions and other psychological factors discussed in Chapter Eighteen.

Investing success is not wholly, nor perhaps not even mainly, a matter of skill in analysing figures. If it were, accountants and finance executives would be the most successful investors. But often they are not because they may lack other qualities such as judgement, the ability to make hard and sometimes unpleasant decisions and the ability to "stick to their guns" when all around them the fallacies of the conventional wisdom are in full flight.

Chapter 16

The Need to
Look Beyond
Traditional
Figures

According to an old saying, the road to hell is paved with good intentions. The road to disappointing investment results is paved with well-intentioned but inadequate or superficial analysis of earnings.

Most attention in specialist recommendations and in the financial media is given to earnings per share and price earnings multiples. So the investing public is generally not fully aware of the importance of a number of other indicators including return on equity and earnings before interest and tax.

Return on equity

This figure is arrived at by dividing earnings after tax and any preference dividends by the amount of shareholders' funds and multiplying by 100 to express it as a percentage. It is a measure of how effectively shareholders' money is being used by the company. The figure can be compared with previous periods to reveal the trend and with comparable figures for the industry to reveal efficiency compared with competitors.

The use of this indicator may show that a company, which at first sight seems to be attractive because earnings per share are rising is not so attractive, because the return on equity is increasing at a lower rate or is declining.

The less impressive performance on the crucial return on equity may reflect that earnings per share though increasing, are increasing at a lower rate than the net equity. That later figure increases as the result of portion of earnings being retained in the business, plus dividends reinvested, plus shares issued in acquisition of other companies or in rights issues offered to shareholders. Investors can feel more confident in buying or continuing to hold shares in which the return on equity is growing steadily.

Earnings before interest and taxation (EBIT)

To go back a stage further and look at what could be called the basic profitability of a company, the earnings before interest and taxation figure is useful. If that figure is not known it can be calculated by adding back onto the net profit after tax, the amount of tax expense and also the net interest expense for the year. That figure is divided by the total assets to express it as a percentage. As the net interest expense figure is not available in some publications it may be necessary to obtain it from your broker's library or from a copy of the financial statements of the company.

The different roles of the return on equity figures and earnings before interest and tax on total assets are as under:

1. **Return on equity** measures how effectively stockholders' money (including capital contributions, and undistributed earnings plus some other items such as reserves and capital profits) is being used.

2. **EBIT rate on total assets** which could be described as a basic profitability indicator measures how effectively the company is using all of the money available to it, including assets which in effect have been financed partly by borrowings and amounts owing to trade creditors.

It is also a means of comparing basic profitability in companies with different situations in these areas:

➤ Gearing, i.e. the extent to which borrowed funds are used

➤ Companies with about the same percentage of borrowed funds which have different interest costs because some borrowed when interest rates were high, others when they were much lower.

➤ Companies in which tax expenses as a percentage of profit before tax differ because of factors such as deductions of losses of previous years, including losses in recently acquired subsidiaries or other special tax factors.

Analysis of earnings components from the EBIT

From an analysis of the earnings before interest and taxation it is possible to ascertain how much of the earnings on shareholders' funds came from normal business operations, how much from taxation benefits and how much from gearing benefits. This matter is covered in Chapter Seventeen.

The problem of unreliable financial statements

Sometimes the financial statements of companies do not report the reality of what has happened during the year. The directors may be able to portray a picture quite different from that which has really happened. They may use convoluted transactions which, by overly legalistic interpretation of some of the fine print in accounting standards, may be seen to comply to those standards.

Or they may achieve their objective of not fully informing the public by using a form of skulduggery which has not yet been covered by the issue of an accounting standard. There have been many instances in recent years where losses were suffered by investors and by creditors of companies because they made their decisions on the basis of the position reported in the financial statements, rather than the reality which was significantly different.

Where to look for possible accounting anomalies

After many years experience in the investment business, in analysing financial statements and earlier experience in an accounting practice, I have been able to develop some ways of locating cases of possible accounting problems. Though there is no one way of trying to track down how financial statements have been distorted, there are some areas of the financial statements, more particularly the notes, which may warrant closer study.

◆ *Capital profits included in revenue*

Sometimes revenue of companies has been inflated by including as revenue, capital gains or "one off gains" which common sense and normal accounting procedures would indicate should not be included as revenue in the profit and loss account. Sometimes, the fact that the tax expense of a company is a good deal lower than would be expected on the basis of profit before tax and the standard company tax rate, could be an indication of this problem, to the extent that the difference is not due to deduction of losses from previous years or other special factors.

◆ *Reserves*

The various reserve accounts are often worth studying. Some company profits have been inflated by the procedure of including as revenue in the profit and loss account, all capital gains made during the period but writing off any losses of that type — not against the profit and loss account but against one of the reserve accounts. A close study of the details in the report concerning reserve accounts is well worthwhile if the difference between the shareholders' funds at the beginning and at the end of the year are not accounted for by retained profits, the receipt of any capital and any capital gain made during the period.

◆ *Accounting standards used*

The notes to the accounts usually contain some details as to the application of accounting standards. Sometimes close scrutiny of these matters may give an indication of items worth further investigation.

Adjustment to normalised earnings

As far as possible, investment analysts, in considering company earnings, try to arrive at what are described as *normalised* earnings. This involves adjusting reported earnings for the effect of items of a special or non-recurring nature such as a debit against earnings of an amount to write off goodwill on acquisitions.

Sometimes these adjustments have been made by analysts from stockbrokers or other institutions in the figures they publish.

Balance sheet items

Most of the comments to date have been on indicators which relate to the profitability of the company. It is also necessary to consider some figures in the balance sheet as an indication of the financial soundness or otherwise of a company. Apart from helping to gauge whether the company is in any danger of failing, an unsound financial position may also indicate the probability of a decline in earnings in times to come.

Sometimes, profits have increased over a period of years simply because of more and more borrowing by the company and the benefit of gearing profits which are described in the next chapter. As that process of more and more gearing cannot continue indefinitely, it can be an indication of a possible decline in earnings when those benefits are no longer available. There may also be the possibility of complete failure in the event of difficult trading conditions.

Proprietorship ratio

Proprietorship ratio is the net equity figure as a percentage of total assets. This figure reflects the percentage of the assets which are financed by shareholders' funds — including capital invested, undistributed profits and capital gains — as distinct from the portion which is, in effect, financed by creditors of various kinds.

A proprietorship ratio of 20 per cent would indicate a fairly highly geared company because liabilities represent 80 per cent of total assets and shareholders' funds only 20 per cent. This could be an indicator of some of the possible problems discussed in previous paragraphs.

Current ratio

Current ratio is the ratio of current assets to current liabilities. Current assets are those which could be expected to be converted into cash in the normal course of business within 12 months. They include items such as cash, accounts receivable, stock on hand and any investments which are readily realisable or fixed-interest investments which are to mature within the next 12 months.

Current liabilities are those liabilities which would involve a payment during the next twelve months. They would include such items as trade creditors, accrued expenses, provision for taxation, short term borrowings of less than 12 months and long term borrowings which are maturing within the next 12 months.

What figure is adequate? In some accounting circles there is a view that it is desirable to have a current asset ratio, i.e. current assets divided by current liabilities, of about 2. This is a somewhat artificial approach because the cash flows of different businesses may vary greatly.

A business which sells most of its goods or services for cash or on seven day credit but has the benefit of 30 days or more for most of its payments to creditors, could generally get by very well on a relatively low current asset ratio. So, too, could those businesses where a large amount is not tied up in stock or work-in-progress which may not be turned into cash for many months. Successful companies of that type may have a current asset ratio a little over 1, or in some cases less than 1.

On the other hand, where cash sales are a small portion of the total, or where a large portion of the sales are on deferred terms, or where receipts from debtors are slow, e.g. in some country areas from time to time, a company could be facing some liquidity problems even if the ratio is fairly close to 2.

♦ *Trends generally more important*

Often it is the trend rather than the absolute figures which is important. If the company has had, for many years, a current ratio of 1.8 and then suddenly it drops to 1.1, this may be a matter of some concern.

Book value per share

This is a measure of the value of assets represented by each share on issue. It is normal practice to exclude from the calculations the value of any intangible assets such as goodwill. The first step in the calculations is to deduct from the amount of net worth the following:

➤ The total of intangible assets

➤ The liquidating or redemption value of any preferred share.

The remainder is divided by the number of shares outstanding.

anservice industries where

◆ *Use of book value per share figures*

By dividing the share price by the book value per share you arrive at the ratio of price to book value which may be of some use in comparing the value of one stock with another, if, all other things were equal, a stock with a lower price to book value per share would be more attractive.

But for that comparison to be valid, you would need to see that all other things really were equal and generally they are far from it in this context. In some service industries where profitability is not so directly related to assets used in the business, a stock with a high price to book value ratio could be better buying than a share in another industry with a lower ratio. There is also the point that what really matters is the earnings and dividends related to share price not the book value.

Relative cost

Though it is not one of the financial ratios usually discussed in relation to profit and loss and balance sheets, the concept of relative cost, which has been discussed elsewhere in the book, is important in analysing company figures. Relative cost is the cost of shares compared with other investments on the basis of the cost of money and interest rates.

Consider for example a company on which the dividend yield at current market price is 3.5 per cent. If the medium term fixed term interest rates were averaging 10 per cent, the relative cost would be 2.9 (10 per cent divided by 3.5 per cent). This is one indicator of whether share prices are high or low. Again, it is not so much the absolute figures which are important but comparison with the trend of figures over a number of years.

Opportunity cost

This is another figure which is not an earnings or financial position indicator which all investors need to understand. In making business and investment decisions, it is important to consider not only costs in the commonly accepted and accounting sense of that term, but in the sense of income or capital gain or other benefits that are foregone as the result of a decision.

♦ *The possible cost of waiting for a recovery*

Sometimes, a decision in the early stages of a cyclical slump to hold for recovery rather than sell at a loss, or at a lower profit than was available previously, may involve the loss of significant income and/or capital gain that could have been earned if the stock were sold and reinvested elsewhere. That opportunity cost can be very large if complete recovery takes eight or ten years or more, as it has in the past.

♦ *Opportunity cost of shares*

For most of the last 20 years, the initial income yield on shares has been well below the income available on bonds, especially when interest rates have been high. That lower initial income is an opportunity cost of investing in shares. For most investors, the superior medium and long term performances of shares, compared with other investments, has more than justified the acceptance of that opportunity cost.

But it is a factor which needs to be considered, especially by retired people or those with limited income from other sources. The much higher opportunity costs of investing in leading stock, or shares with low or no dividend yields could make it desirable for them to look to shares which provide a higher initial dividend yield and so involve a lower opportunity cost.

♦ *Example of opportunity cost*

If you are unfamiliar with the opportunity cost concept this example may make it a little clearer. On a war-time island base some Australian servicemen were able to purchase beer at their canteen for the very low price of 10¢ per bottle. US troops in a neighbouring camp, who did not have the right to buy at that canteen, offered the Australian servicemen up to $1.50 per bottle.

Some of the Australians who normally liked to drink beer found those offers too tempting and sold to the Americans. For the Australians, the outlay cost of the beer was 10¢ per bottle. But the opportunity cost of drinking it rather than selling to the Americans was $1.50.

Chapter 17

Going Beyond
Conventional Analysis
to the Components
of Earnings

Need for analysis

Though most investment recommendations and media comment on shares go no further than earnings per share and dividends per share figures, the point was made in Chapter Sixteen that, for sound analysis, it is necessary to go further into return on equity and some other indicators.

The quality of analysis can be improved even further by analysing the components of return on equity into hard core earnings and earnings from other sources. The hard core earnings figures may give a better idea of trend in earnings and probable growth in earnings than the total return on equity, including returns from other sources which may be non-recurring.

Components of return on equity

The components of return on equity to be analysed are as under:

➤ Hard core earnings, i.e. earnings from basic business operations

➤ Earnings from gearing benefits

➤ Earnings from tax benefits.

The nature of each of these components and their significance is discussed below.

Hard core earnings

The hard core earnings, or earnings from basic operations, are the component of return on equity which comes from the basic business of providing goods or services to customers.

◆ *Significance*

This component represents what the return on equity would have been if there had been no benefits from gearing and no tax benefits. As it is some of the later sources of return on equity which may be non-recurring, there could be a case for caution about stocks in which the hard core earnings are relatively small compared with the other components.

Earnings from gearing benefits

This component of return on equity measures the benefits that come from the fact that part of the total cost of assets used in the business are financed from sources other than shareholders' funds, namely from borrowings and trade creditors. It is the excess of the earning rate on assets above the net cost of funds from borrowers and trade creditors.

Remember that of the various items on the liabilities side of a balance sheet not all of them involve an interest cost. For example, the considerable portion of total funds that represents the amount owing to trade creditors does not involve any interest cost. Accruals and provisions for such items as taxation are also without interest cost.

So the net interest cost as a percentage of total liabilities is generally much lower than normal borrowing rates.

◆ *Significance*

This measure is significant in many ways. It may show, for example, in periods such as 1992 and 1993, that lower interest rates may have been a significant contributor to return on equity. If the large reduction in interest rates is not likely to recur in later periods, or if a long downward trend in interest rates is followed by an increase, as happened in 1994, gearing benefits in future, may be lower with a resultant decrease, or smaller increase in return on equity and earnings per share.

Similarly, the emergence of a trend towards high interest rates could be expected to have a significant adverse effect on those companies where gearing benefits make up a sizeable portion of total return on equity.

Another more significant point is that analysis of a company with a rapidly growing gearing benefit figure may show that borrowings have been increasing rapidly. That could mean troubles in the event of rising interest rates. As well as the adverse effect on earnings from such a development, it could mean greatly increased financial risk — the risk of serious financial problems, especially if a period of increased interest rates and a need to re-finance debt coincides with difficult trading conditions.

Sometimes even if the probability of serious financial problems may not be acute, increased return on equity and earnings per share from increased borrowing may be unlikely to continue. The trend towards higher and higher borrowings cannot continue indefinitely at a fast rate.

A company which initially has low borrowings has, for a time considerable scope for increased gearing benefits, return on equity and earnings per share. It may increase its liabilities as a percentage of total assets from 25 per cent to 50 per cent or 60 per cent. But, ultimately, a point is reached where the expansion of borrowings and total liabilities must taper off — either due to reluctance of creditors to provide more funds, or from a self-imposed limit by the board in the interest of financial risk being kept within tolerable limits.

So at the very time when so many analysts are making confident recommendations for the stock on the higher earnings per share, the reality is that for subsequent periods with no increase in gearing benefits, if, all other things are equal, the high rate of increase in earnings per share over the last few years would not continue.

Tax benefits

This measures the portion of return on equity which comes from tax benefits, namely the fact that the tax expense of the company is lower than normal. Normal tax is the figure obtained by applying the standard rate of company tax to the profit before tax.

The tax benefit may arise from a number of causes such as special depreciation or investment allowances, the fact that the tax impact on profits earned outside Australia may be lower, or from the deduction of losses of previous years.

♦ *Significance*

Depending on the particular nature of the items which produced the tax benefit, they may be non recurring. If that is so, then a lower rate of growth, or perhaps a decline in return on equity and earnings per share, could be expected in later years.

Calculation of components

With that description of the three components we now turn to the way in which they are calculated. As return on equity is based on net profit after tax (see Chapter Sixteen), it is necessary to use after-tax figures in these calculations.

One way is to make the detailed calculations for the three components. A simpler way, is to calculate the hard core earnings and tax benefits and then deduct the total of those two components from total earnings on equity to arrive at the earning rate from gearing benefits.

♦ *Example of calculations*

This approach can be seen by working through an example of a company.

Profit and loss figures — The relevant figures in the Profit and Loss Account in millions of dollars are shown below.

	$(m)
Net Profit before tax	21.9
Tax expense	1.5
Net profit after tax	20.4
Net interest expense	34.5

Balance Sheet figures — The relevant figures in the Balance Sheet are as under:

	$(m)
Net equity or Shareholders' Funds	120
Total Liabilities	355
Total Assets	475

Calculation of basic data

A preliminary step is to arrive at some basic figures which are needed in the calculations.

➤ **Return on equity** — Divide net profit after tax, i.e. $20.4 million by net equity, i.e. $120 million and multiply by 100 to express it as a percentage which works out at 17.0 per cent.

➤ **Normal tax** — Multiply profit before tax, i.e. $21.9 million by standard company tax rate of 33 per cent which works out at $7.2 million.

➤ **Primary profitability** — profit before interest and tax — Two steps are involved:
   ▪ First add to profit before tax, i.e. $21.9 million, the net interest, i.e. $34.5 million to arrive at the profit before interest and tax of $56.4 million.
   ▪ Second divide that last figure, i.e. $56.4 million by total assets, i.e. $475 million and multiply by 100 to arrive at the earning rate of profit before interest and tax which is 11.87 per cent.

Calculation of earnings components

With that data we can now proceed to calculate the three components of earnings.

◆ *Hard core earnings*

1. First write down the figure of 11.87 per cent calculated in the second last paragraph above.

2. To allow for the impact of tax at standard rates multiply that figure by 0.67, (the proportion of earnings remaining after standard tax rate of 33 per cent or 0.33). That calculation produces a figure of 7.95 per cent.

As that is the figure which would have been the return on equity had there been no gearing or tax benefits, it is the hard core earnings rate from business operations.

♦ *Tax benefits*

1. From the normal tax cost, i.e. at standard rates, i.e. the figure of $7.2 million calculated as shown above, deduct the actual tax expense figure of $1.5 million which gives a tax benefit of $5.7 million.

2. Divide that last figure of $5.7 million by the net equity figure of $120 million and multiply by 100 to express it as a percentage. This gives the tax benefit figure of 4.75 per cent.

♦ *Gearing benefits*

As we now have the total return on equity, the hard core business operations component and the tax benefit, we can arrive at the gearing benefit as under.

Total return on equity as calculated above is of which	17.00%
Hard core earnings figure is	7.95%
Tax benefit is	4.75%
to make a total for those two items of	12.70%
So the gearing benefit component is	4.30%

Summary of analysis

The contribution of the three components to return on equity is summarised in the table overleaf.

Component	Earning Rate	Percentage of Total
Hard core earnings	7.95%	46.80%
Tax benefit	4.75%	27.90%
Gearing benefit	4.30%	25.30%
Total	17.0%	100.00%

This summary shows that a little under half of total earnings came from the hard core business operations and about a quarter each from the other two components of tax benefit and gearing benefit.

In considering the impact of the above figures, the first point to note is the contribution from tax benefit — 27.9 per cent of the total return on equity. If further study shows that the factors which produced the tax benefit are unlikely to continue, a decline of up to a quarter in return on equity, and possibly on dividends, may be likely.

That could be significant to the investor both from the viewpoint of the reduced income and possible reduced share price (or a lower rate of growth in share prices). There could be a third possible effect of any significant reduction in earnings, namely the market pricing the stock at a lower market rating — for example reducing the rating from 1.5 times to 1.2 times the market average.

As for benefit from gearing, that would be of concern if the contribution from that source were a higher percentage of total equity. So, too, would it be a concern if study showed that rising interest rates seemed likely to reduce that component and hence total return on equity or that changed conditions may reduce the opportunity for borrowings.

Minor imperfections in above approach

The above analysis is very useful in detecting the essential nature of the profitability of a company, and in answering important questions about the source of earnings, and the extent to which future earnings may be affected by the non continuance of tax benefits or gearing benefits.

On highly theoretical grounds, it could be criticised in that it does not deduct certain costs associated with the activities which have produced gearing or tax benefits. But from a practical point of view, that objection is not a problem. If the relevant costs were segregated they would probably not be very significant.

Moreover, the purpose of the analysis is not to determine to several decimal places the earning rate from various sources. It is to give a broad indication of the proportion of earnings that come from the various sources. In some cases, appropriate adjustments may be necessary for interests of minority shareholders or preference dividends.

Warning of serious problems ahead

This type of analysis is of more than academic interest. Apart from making it possible to better estimate future growth in return on equity, this type of analysis has been very helpful in giving warnings of companies likely to get into serious trouble. A high return on equity, as the result of higher and higher gearing, and non recurring tax benefits has been a characteristic of many high flying companies in the years before they crashed.

Chapter 18

How the Herd
Mentality and Mob
Psychology Affect
the Stock Market

"Extraordinary delusions and the madness of crowds"

A book with the above title would not be seen in the lists of prescribed or recommended texts for college courses in investment or finance over the last 30 years. That is a great pity. If that book had been featured in more of those courses, the efficient market hypothesis would probably not have gained so many devoted adherents among academics, students, and practitioners.

Readers may recall the quote from George Soros in Chapter One to the effect that the more people believe in the efficient market hypothesis, the more unstable markets become.

The interesting point about that book, a later edition of which was published by Harmony Books New York in 1980, was that it was written in 1841 by Charles Mackay LL.D. Its 700 pages encompass a wide range of mass mania and crowd behaviour including the South Sea Bubble in England in the early eighteenth century and the tulip mania in Holland in the seventeenth century when a crazy boom pushed the price of a single tulip bulb up to the equivalent of tens of thousands of dollars in today's money.

The 1980 edition includes a foreword by a highly respected modern investment specialist and author, Andrew Tobias. It refers to the foreword of an earlier 1931 edition by Baruch who wrote of the period of dizzily spiralling stock prices in the boom before the 1929 crash:

> " ... *if .... we had all continuously repeated 'two and two still make four   much of the evil might have been averted"*

Andrew Tobias also referred to spiralling stock prices in the late 1960s when synergy was the new magic word which:

> *"meant, in essence that two and two could, under astute management equal five. It was alchemy of a sort and enough to drive at least one stock, in two years, from $6 a share to $140. The talk of the town. Not much later it sold for $1."*

His magnificent foreword to Charles Mackay's book concluded with this paragraph

> *"Once upon a time there was an emperor with no clothes. For the longest time no one noticed. As you will read in this marvellous book, there have been many naked emperors since. There will be doubtless many more."*

Little wonder that many intelligent people are bemused so often by the sight of investment people acting just like a mob of cattle or sheep rushing madly this way and that.

The vast difference between theory and reality

According to many people in the investment business, the present is always a good time to buy shares. If shares have risen sharply, the fact that they have done so well is seen as a good reason for buying so that you can enjoy a continuation of that rise. If they are much lower than they were in the recent past, that decline is put forward as a reason why you will never find a better time than now to buy.

Most of the conventional wisdom seems to be based on the myth that the preordained state of affairs is for the share market to rise constantly. Any decline is seen as a temporary mental aberration from which the market will soon recover before returning to its upward path.

The reality is vastly different. Apart from the impact of market cycles discussed earlier, there are from time to time common stock investments that are affected by the psychological excesses to which Andrew Tobias and Baruch have referred.

♦ *The film "Wall Street"*

The situation when the boom mentality takes over was well summed up in a five word comment by one character in the film *Wall Street*:

"The illusion becomes the reality."

So for sound investment it is necessary to recognise that market prices and hence the result of share investments can be affected very greatly by psychological factors, the herd mentality and mob psychology. It may be easier to appreciate this point if you know something of the way in which various sections of the investment industry react to the realities of the market.

The various players in this mutual self-delusion

What happens in the share market could be described as large scale mutual self-delusion. It is myths about constant upward market trend rather than the realities which are the subject matter at most meetings and conferences and social gatherings when investment people get together.

The realist, the person who is courageous enough to point out at various times that share prices are dangerously high, is seen in a way as "letting the side down". It is not the done thing to be bearish.

In 1987, and again at the end of 1993, when I was warning that a share market slump was imminent and that a decline could be very severe, I was one of a small minority.

Few investment discussions even mention the existence of cycles which, in fact, are so important for the share investor. Even the possibility of a cyclical decline when prices are high is brushed aside as not likely to happen. The realist who studies past behaviour of share prices and raises questions when prices are high is seen as unfashionable.

Indeed, people like myself have often been described as "doom-sayers". (If you are ever making up a dictionary of investment terms you could include the definition of doom-sayer as a person who speaks the truth and dares to disagree with the conventional wisdom.)

Perhaps it is an illustration of that old saying that when ignorance is bliss 'tis folly to be wise. When so many people in the investment business are doing well out of perpetuating the myth that share prices more or less move constantly upward, it is not surprising that the realists tend to be in the minority.

Unlike other industries, there seems to be little interest in trying to find out what causes incorrect decisions or incorrect recommendations for people who go into the market when prices were already high. It is fortunate for the community that other professions act in a somewhat different way. For example, if the engineers followed the same sort of never-questioning-the-past attitude, the collapse of a bridge built in a certain way would not be followed by an attempt to find out what went wrong but by continuing to repeat faulty methods of construction elsewhere.

Wanted — a baloney or "blue sky" index

What we really need is what may be described as a baloney or "blue sky" index as a means of calculating, at any time, how much money is pouring into the market and hence pushing prices up as the result of inadequate or misleading information. Perhaps the solution is to combine the modern technique of remote sensing through a satellite, computers and a modified polygraph, (a polygraph you may recall is the instrument to record heart beats and respiratory movements which is sometimes used as a lie detector).

It would have to be modified in some way to reflect not only those who are deliberately telling lies but those who are repeating seriously incorrect statements, many of which tend to be accepted as true. Perhaps it could be called a Goebbeling detector, namely a detector of untrue statements which have been repeated for so long that they are accepted as true.

An example is false statements that blue chips hold their value in a slump and that you can't go wrong in quality stocks with good earnings prospects. If everybody involved in advising on shares had to wear one of these Goebbeling adjusted polygraphs which was also able to record the success or otherwise of those statements on the listener, that would be a start. If they could be beamed in some way up to a satellite and then down to computers which could tabulate and summarise them, it would extremely useful.

We would then have an indicator of the amount of blue sky or exaggeration or baloney which is persuading people to put money into the share market or into equity trusts, as distinct from those factors which so many investment theories suggest are the sole determinants of market behaviour.

How facts can be rationalised away

There is another factor which leads to market prices for considerable periods being affected more by the herd instinct and mob psychology than by fundamental factors. It is the ability of so many people in the investment industry to rationalise away those facts which do not fit in with the underlying belief that it is always a good time to buy shares.

Many people, in many areas of life, are affected by this approach of "I have made up my mind, don't try to confuse me with the facts", but none do it so well as those involved with the stock market.

The temptation to overlook relative costs and opportunity costs

Sometimes the mob psychology impact on market prices takes the form of forgetting the importance of relative cost and opportunity cost. For example, people have been persuaded at various times to buy stocks because dividend yields or price earnings multiples are attractive compared to various periods in the past. But, if you look to the more objective comparison, namely the relative cost of shares as measured by dividend yields in relation to interest rates, you may find that stock prices are not nearly as cheap as the superficial analysis related solely to dividend yields or price earning multiples may suggest.

The failure to take into account opportunity cost is another example of failure to accept reality.

How to avoid being trampled by the herd

Until something like the Goebbeling polygraph referred to above is available, there is no precise way of knowing how much baloney or blue sky is in the market at a particular time. Incidentally, if that information were available the smart course would be not to leave the share market immediately, simply because the blue sky share component was high, because it may continue in that state for some considerable time. It may even go on to higher levels with an even greater blue sky component. To ensure that the gains you make in the share market are not eroded by significant slumps when, for whatever reason, the blue sky component suddenly decreases greatly in a slump, the following steps may be helpful:

➤ Gradually adjust the portion of your capital in the market according to an assessment of the position of the share market on the basis of factors such as prices related to the long term trend and its relative cost, (i.e. dividend yield compared with interest rates) and whether a cyclical slump may be about due or overdue on the normal time pattern.

➤ If the share market or a particular stock has risen in price so much that you would not be very keen to buy into the market or into that stock at that price, think seriously about whether you should be selling a portion of your holding.

➤ Be very wary when, in response to a question about whether prices may be high in a bull market, the conventional wisdom assures you that "things are different this time". In the six booms and slumps which I have been through in the last 40 years, that is always said when prices reach dangerous levels. But, in effect, things are really not different and the boom and high prices are invariably followed by a slump. That has been the experience in every boom since the South Sea Bubble 250 years ago.

➤ Remember the importance of relative cost and opportunity cost discussed above and in earlier chapters.

➤ Do not be lulled into a false sense of complacency by people telling you that prices may decline a little but it will be a healthy technical correction. That was the initial knee-jerk reaction to a number of price declines which turned into severe slumps which lasted for many years.

➤ Assess your position carefully when you see evidence that prices may be nearing the end of the boom, such as those factors discussed in Chapter Thirteen, and signs of excessive enthusiasm for the market in terms of a great increase in the number of new companies being floated.

➤ Finally, remember the step system which enables you to make decisions in stages by initially buying or selling part of your planned purchases or sales of a particular stock or in the market overall and then watching the market very closely for the timing of any further buying or selling.

Benefiting from psychological factors

For most investors, one very important aspect of the mob psychology and herd mentality is to beware that they are not caught up in the enthusiasm so that they move into the market or increase their shareholdings when those forces have pushed prices up to levels from which a severe decline is almost inevitable. But a knowledge of this may also help investors benefit from those factors by taking advantage of it in their buying and selling decisions.

For example, a stock which may not appear good buying on objective grounds, may be attractive because the psychological factors could push prices up considerably. So it is possible to take advantage of this by retaining for a time part of your holding of the stock — subject to the step system of making some partial sale in case there is a sudden fall, and then watching market developments closely for the timing of further sales.

These factors may also be relevant in relation to new company flotations. The hype surrounding the public offering, as well as promotion by underwriters and others, could result in the stock opening at a price well above the issue price. This can provide quick profits for the fleet of foot, but are disappointing for those who hold too long.

A classic example of that situation was the flotation some years ago of Breakwater Trust, the operators of the Townsville casino. Anything but a superficial study of the prospectus showed that the projected earnings figures were over-optimistic. So it was not attractive as a medium or long term investment.

But it was also fairly clear that the share issue would be very popular mainly because it followed the highly successful flotation of Jupiters, the Gold Coast casino. So it was likely that on listing, the shares would open at a significant premium to issue price before subsequently declining.

So the investors who did their homework properly sold part of their holding soon after listing at a high profit and then the balance at a profit of about 80 per cent when a buying frenzy pushed prices up to high point which was unlikely to be maintained. A little later the price declined sharply. For the last 10 years it has been way below issue price and early in 1995 was about half the issue price.

To summarise, some company flotations may be attractive both for "stag" profits, by selling at a premium shortly after listing and as medium to long term investments. But remember there is a risk associated with any share investment, and especially the possibility of a serious overall market decline between purchasing the stock and its opening trades. That risk becomes higher if the market is already high, e.g. in Zones 1 or 2 relating to average dividend yield.

Consider Behavioural Finance

Remember to consider the points made and the research done by behavioural finance people including the effects of fads and fashions on stock markets which are covered in the papers in the book *Advances In Behavioural Finance* to which reference is made in Chapter One.

Impact of psychological factors on particular stocks or industries

It is not only the overall share market which is affected by the herd mentality and mob psychology. From time to time, there are stampedes into and out of particular stocks or particular industries due to a number of factors to which we now turn.

Glamour stocks or industries of the month or year

Sometimes particular stocks or particular industries seem to be surrounded by an aura of glamour. This led to the frantic boom in particular types of stocks, such as the example quoted in the reference to Andrew Tobias earlier.

This phenomenon is not limited to Australia but can be seen in markets all over the world. In the Australian market in the frantic 1969 boom which attracted great international interest, a nickel exploration stock, Poseidon rose from less than $1.00 to $280.00 before declining to zero. It led to a boom both in mineral exploration stocks and later to all mining stocks including a number of market leaders.

The slump after that boom resulted in a decline of about 70 per cent in the leading stocks, and about 40 per cent in the rest of the market. The reaction to the boom in mineral stocks was so prolonged that, despite several rises which were not sustained, the relevant index at the beginning of 1993 — 23 years later — was no higher than at the end of 1969.

From time to time, high technology stocks have become glamour stocks which have pushed prices up to levels way above those which they would have reached on their intrinsic merits.

Effect of cult figures and public relations

Sometimes the prices of stocks of particular companies go up to extremely high levels because of a mistaken belief that the chief executive officer has some sort of Midas touch which will make riches for the shareholders. Sometimes this belief is based on good results in the past or the fact that the chief executive officer is a highly visible public figure.

Sometimes there is a tendency for people in the investment industry to look at these companies and their prospects through very rose tinted glasses, partly because of general enthusiasm and partly because it may be good business to look favourably on these companies from which business of various kinds may be expected.

Often the very feature which produces a lot of the favourable publicity, namely the rapid expansion of these businesses, is the very factor which would make an objective analyst considerably less enthusiastic about them. Too rapid expansion of companies has been a common feature of many of the dramatic company failures.

It seems that the public relations success of these companies created the belief that they had some particular magic in making profits. That must be the explanation for so many institutions losing so heavily in these companies when objective analysis some years before their fall would have shown that there were serious question marks and a strong case for selling.

A false belief that high growth will continue for ever

There is an old saying that nothing succeeds like success. In the stock market this could be modified to say that nothing succeeds like success — for a time. Many investors have suffered severe losses because they believed, or had been persuaded by advisers to believe, that the rapid rate of growth in earnings and share prices of a company in the past would continue indefinitely.

The reality is that very few, if any, companies are able to maintain a high rate of growth in earnings and a high rate of growth in share prices indefinitely. Some of them have been able to maintain rates well above average for a very long period. But it is almost a law of nature that the spectacular rates of growth will not be continued.

The riches-to-rags-to-riches story of BHP share prices over the last 27 years was outlined in Chapter Three. Another classic example is BTR Nylex. Between 1982 and 1990 when the share price increased by a spectacular 3400 per cent it seemed to be the share of the century. Since 1991 it has declined by about 30 per cent in contrast to the rise of above 20 per cent in the All Ordinaries Index.

Psychological factors and recovery stocks

The psychological impact on stock prices also needs to be considered in buying recovery stocks, i.e. stocks which have previously been doing very well but have fallen from grace. It has been said with some truth that the market has a long memory. Often stocks with very good earnings records which have then blotted their copy book, so to speak, with reduced earnings for a year or two, have taken a long time to regain anything like the market rating they had prior to their fall.

This means that even if objective analysis shows that earnings and dividends are increasing, that increase may not be fully reflected in increase in stock prices. The reason is that, because of their fall from grace, the market may afford them a lower market rating for some time to come. This means that when you are buying recovery stocks you need to consider the following matters:

➤ Does a thorough analysis suggest that the company has really turned the corner and that current earnings will be maintained and hopefully increased in the future?

➤ Is the overall stock market pattern such that the increase in earnings of this company, and indeed other companies, will be reflected by increased stock prices and not offset by reaction to previous excessive enthusiasm?

➤ Are there any signs that the market is gradually restoring to the stock the higher market rating which it enjoyed in the past, (remember market rating is the price of the stock measured by dividend yield or price earnings multiple related to the market average)?

Remember that psychological factors may have a greater impact on the result of your investment than what happens in the individual company. When buying stocks for recovery, what you need to buy is not just stocks which are likely to report increased earnings and dividends but stocks which will achieve an increase in market price.

Chapter 19

Prudent Use
of Options and
Futures Trading

If you are a crafty politician you always contrive to leave your options open, so that when you sniff a change in the political winds you are not prevented from adopting an alternative course.

For investors, options and futures trading can be a means of increasing their returns from share investment.

Various uses of options

Options can be used by investors in a number of different ways, namely:

➤ **Trading** — A sophisticated means of short term trading for those investors with some skills in this area.

➤ **Speculating on margins** — Maximising profits if your judgement is correct by the use of gearing in something like the same ways as it applies in negative gearing.

➤ **Facilitating purchase of shares** — Ensuring that stock can be bought at some time in the future at a specified price rather than the higher price which you believe may be applicable at that time.

➤ **Downside protection** — The use of put options is a form of insurance protection against a serious decline in share values which may be imminent.

➤ **Increase in returns** — By adding additional income through the selling or writing of options on stocks in your portfolio.

➤ **Reducing transaction costs** — To obtain the benefits of an increase you expect in the overall share market by purchase of options rather than purchase of individual stocks with greater transaction costs, brokerage, etc.

Before going on to discuss the various ways in which options can be used, it is necessary to know how options operate. It is to that subject to which we now turn.

What options are all about

Most investors would be familiar with options over property. For example, the developer wishing to buy a number of small blocks to aggregate them into a larger site for redevelopment, does not wish to outlay a large amount initially on the purchase of individual smaller blocks. The problem could be that if three of the four blocks are acquired and it is not possible to acquire the fourth block, a large amount may be invested in what is virtually dead capital.

If options can be obtained over each of the blocks, then, even if the purchase price is a little higher than normal, the developer does not have to make any large outlays until all of the blocks are acquired. If they are not acquired, the options on the blocks that have been acquired would be allowed to lapse. The net cost would be a great deal less than if the properties had been purchased, which would have involved not only purchase price but the costs of buying and subsequently selling, including legal costs, commission, etc, and possible capital loss if market values were to decline.

So an option essentially is a right to buy, and sometimes to sell, an asset at an agreed price at a future date. Options traded on the stock exchange are controlled and subject to the regulations of the Australian Options Market which, in effect, is a subsidiary of the Australian Stock Exchange.

Call options are options which give the buyer the right, but not the obligation, to buy shares at an agreed price, i.e. the exercise price, at any time up to the end of a specified period.

Put options give the right to the holder to sell stock at an agreed price, i.e. the exercise price, at any time up to the end of a specified period.

Option premiums are the amounts paid by the buyer to the seller for the right to buy or sell the relevant stock. It is customary to describe the seller as the *writer* of the options and the act of selling an option as *writing* an option.

Option stocks are currently those 40 stocks on which options may be traded. Just which stocks are in this category can be seen by looking at the list of option trading in newspapers, such as the *Australian*, *Sydney Morning Herald* and *Australian Financial Review*.

Exercise price is the range of prices at which trading in options on specific stocks is possible. For example, on 3 March 1995, the last sale price of BHP shares was at $18.44. At that time call options were quoted for exercise prices from $14.00 to $22.00 for maturities up to the end of December 1995 and from $15.00 up to $23.00 for longer maturities.

Underlying stock prices — The exercise price referred to above is the price at which call options to buy and put options to sell can be exercised. That price should be distinguished from the underlying price of the stock, namely the price at which the stock is trading which, as indicated above, in the case of BHP on 3 March 1995 was $18.44.

Period covered — For most stocks on which options trading is possible there are contracts expiring up to nine months ahead. Options on different stocks have different cycles.

"In the money" options — A call option is said to be in the money if the exercise price is lower than the price at which the underlying stock is selling. In the above example, with BHP stocks selling at $18.44, options with an exercise price of $15.00 to $18.00 would be in the money.

"Out of the money" options are call options in which the exercise price is higher than the underlying price of the stock. In the BHP example the options with an exercise price of $18.50 and above would be out of the money.

"At the money" options are options in which the exercise price equals the underlying price of the stock. Because the price of the stock may move in 1¢ or 2¢ or 3¢ stages and the options in 25¢ or 50¢ steps, it is only when the price at which the stock is selling happens to coincide with one of the steps in the option prices that there would be an "at the money" option.

Size of contract — Each contract is for one thousand shares.

◆ *Open positions*

The figures shown in newspapers as the total open positions show the number of contracts which are open at that time. An option contract is open until it is either exercised by the holder, or expires at the end of the relevant period, or is closed out.

◆ *Closing out*

The holder of a position in the options market closes out his position by selling a contract with the same exercise price and maturity date. Shareholders who have written or sold a call option against shares which they are holding to increase their return from shares, may close out their position by buying a call option at a similar exercise price and maturity date. For example, they may wish to sell the underlying shares, either because they need the cash or because they may feel that a large decline in prices is imminent. In that event, one of the alternatives for them is to buy a call option with a similar exercise price and similar maturity date. That closes out or cancels the option which they have written and enables them to have the shares which have temporarily been transferred into the name of the clearing house back into their name.

A person who writes or sells an option against stock which he is holding, deposits a share certificate or arranges for an electronic transfer of the relevant number of stocks into the clearing house of the Australian Options Market to ensure that if that option is exercised the scrip is available. It is also possible to write options by depositing the relevant amount of cash with the clearing house.

◆ *Exercise of options*

Only a relatively small portion of options are exercised. If at the end of the option period the price of the stock is below the option price, then obviously the holder of a call option would not exercise it. But the fact that the price of the underlying stock has risen above the exercise price of a call option does not necessarily mean that it will be immediately exercised. The holder may prefer to continue to hold the option in the expectation that, as the rise in share prices continues, the value of his option in the Options Market will also rise (not necessarily by the same amount, see discussion later on trading of options).

When a call option is exercised the Australian Options Market selects by random process from all of the writers or sellers of call options at that exercise price, the holder against whom the option will be exercised.

American-type options are options which can be exercised at any time up to the maturity date. This is the type of option which is traded in the Australian Options Market. **European-type options** are options which can be exercised only on the maturity date of the option. Options which have been issued by some companies to the shareholders which are traded on the Stock Exchange are European type options which can be exercised only on the specified maturity date.

◆ *Treatment of dividends*

Any dividends paid on a stock during the period covered by an option goes to the holder of the shares and not to the holder of the option. Sometimes, and for some holders, the pending payment of a dividend may be a factor in deciding whether or not they should exercise the option — particularly if the dividend is relatively high and is fully entitled to the dividend tax credit.

◆ *Changes in underlying shares*

The exercise price of an option is adjusted for any changes which affect the underlying stock, such as bonus issues, share splits, or other factors. Adjustment is made so that, other things being equal, the parties to the option transaction are in the same position as they would have been before that change.

The factors that affect option prices

There has been extensive study of the mathematics of options trading. Various models have been developed to explain the way in which option prices are likely to vary.

These formulae recognise the following six variables:

➤ **Spot price** — the price at which the stock is currently trading.

➤ **Exercise or strike price** — the price at which the option may be exercised.

➤ **Time to expiry** — the period from the current date to the maturity date of the option, which is the last date which it can be exercised, generally expressed as a decimal part of a year.

➤ **Interest rate** — the short term interest rate which measures the opportunity cost of holding the option rather than earning interest on the amount invested in the purchase of the option.

➤ **Dividends** — which are expected to be paid during the period covered by the option.

➤ **Volatility** — the volatility of the underlying stock covered by the option.

Of the above six factors, all of them except volatility are known. From formulae which have been developed by studies over the years and which would generally be available from stockbrokers dealing in options, it is possible to calculate the *implied volatility*. This is the volatility which is implied on the basis of the price or premium at which options are traded.

In the options market, volatility to some extent, serves the same purpose as dividend yields and price earnings multiple in the share market in that it enables a comparison of option prices for different stocks with different prices or different expiry dates. In general, stock with low volatility would suggest that the option is relatively cheap and high volatility that it is relatively expensive.

Liquidity is another factor which has to be considered. It can be gauged by looking at the level of open interest or open positions (see comment above) and the daily turnover in the relevant option series (option on the particular stock at the particular exercise price with the particular maturity date). Generally, there is higher liquidity in options which are at the money or close to it and are more or less midway along the time scale, i.e. not too close and not too far from the expiry date.

There are three measures which can help in making options trading decisions. They are referred to by letters of the Greek alphabet, namely delta, gamma and theta.

Delta is the sensitivity of an options premium or price to a small change in the spot share price, i.e. the price of the underlying stock.

Gamma is the sensitivity of the delta of an option (as described above) to a small change in the spot share price.

Theta is the sensitivity of the price of an option or premium to a small change in the time to expiry of the option.

Obviously the above three factors are a fairly sophisticated means of considering some of the variability factors that affect option prices. The underlying factor, of course, is the way in which the price of the underlying stock moves. For example, if you buy an option on BHP shares at the price of $19.00 when they are currently trading at $18.44, you are expecting some upward price movement. If the day after you purchase the option there happened to be an overall share market decline, or any other factor which caused BHP share prices to decline from $18.44 to $17.00 or $16.00 and to stay at that level for the whole of the period until the expiry date of the option, then, in the language of the classics, "you have done your dough". In financial markets, no matter how sophisticated your approach may be, no matter how careful your analysis, if your judgement is wrong it can cost you money.

Understanding published information about options

Though several major newspapers publish some details of option prices, the information in the *Australian Financial Review* is the most comprehensive. The following comments explain the significance of the information.

The information is published for all of the stocks in which options can be written. One section deals with call options and the other deals with put options. In the *Australian Financial Review* of 6 March 1995, looking at the section under call options relating to BHP, it shows that the last sale price on 3 March 1995 was $18.44.

Details are shown for the series of options maturing in March, June, September and December 1995 and March and September 1996. For each of those periods there is a range of strike prices for different levels. The third, fourth and fifth columns of the table are comparable to the tables of stock prices in that they show the "buyer", the "seller" and the last sale. The next column shows the volume of contracts and the seventh column shows the open interest (see comments above).

The next two columns show the implied volatility (see comments above based on both the buyer price and on the seller price). The second last column shows the delta (see comments above) for the options.

As the last sale price was $18.44, the nearest strike price to that figure at which options can be bought is $18.50. If we look at the figures on that line for March 1995 maturity we see there was a "buyer" quotation of 37¢, "seller" quotation of 40¢ and the last sale price of 38¢. The volume of sales was 58,400 and there is an open interest of 5,467. Turning to implied volatility which was discussed above, we find that the implied volatility on the buyer price is 17.2 per cent per annum and on the seller price 18.7 per cent per annum.

In the second last column we see the delta as .53. Generally, for options at or close to being at the money (strike price being equal to or close to the last sale price) the delta is generally around .50. The final column shows the estimated annual return on the purchase of options. The figure there is 34.45 per cent.

Whether that return is achieved, of course, would depend on subsequent development.

For a person considering trading in options, most brokers would be able to provide more information, including the figures for gamma and theta (see comments above) which are not published in the *Financial Review*. For those who are trading in options (getting the benefit of gearing as explained above) generally the best call option to buy is an option which is "at the money" or close to it.

That option tends to give greatest possible benefit from share price increases and the greatest protection from a share price fall. Traders can use the delta figure as an indication of the probability that the option will be exercised, the sensitivity of the option value to changes in the price of the underlying share and an indication of how many shares the option-holder has potential control over at that stage. It may also be used as a hedge ratio to indicate how many shares to buy or sell to remove any risk.

Experienced traders find the delta useful as a guide to the extent of their exposure and as a help in hedging. It can also be used by them to calculate a net position and as a trading guide.

After considering the information published in the *Australian Financial Review* and further information available from a broker, experienced options traders would generally prefer to buy low volatility and sell low volatility. They would also keep an eye on their liquidity and would generally avoid trading in stocks which are not liquid and where there is a wide spread between the bid and offer prices. As indicated in comments above, liquidity tends to be higher when the published level of open interest is relatively high, the daily turnover in the series is significant, the options are close to or at the money, and are not too close or far away from expiry date.

In the description of the operation of options in the early part of this chapter, it may have seemed that when the market moves the right way, the holders of call options would exercise their options, buy the shares at the strike price which would then be lower than the market price, with the intention of selling to realise a profit, or to hold the shares at a lower price than would have been available if they had not used the call option. In practice, many traders find it more convenient and more profitable not to exercise their option even when they are well in the money, i.e. price of the stock is well above the exercise price. Instead, they may sell the option they hold at an enhanced price.

As share prices rise and the spot price moves further above the exercise price, then the value of the call option would depend on the delta. If the delta is .5, a rise of 50¢ in the share price would generally be accompanied by a rise of 25¢ in the price of the option.

Simulated exposure to holding shares

Some purchasers of options use the options to simulate the position they would be in if they were holding a particular share or the whole market.

In a book entitled *Equity Options* by Hugh Denning, the point is made on page 78, that a simple long call position to simulate an exposure to a particular stock should outperform holding the relevant stocks.

Selling options against stock in a portfolio

Having looked at trading in share options which, as indicated earlier, is a type of gearing with some of the features of negative gearing investment, we can now look at the more conservative use of options. Investors who have a share portfolio which includes stocks on which options are traded, may consider the selling or writing of options as a means of increasing the return on their share investment.

Because most options are not exercised, there is a good probability that this process will give the shareholder the benefit of the premium received on the sale or the writing of his option, and still enable him to continue to hold the shares.

If there is a large rise in the share price and the option is exercised, the seller, or writer, of the option is still in good shape. If an option is written at an out of the money price, for example, at $19.50 when the share price is $18.44, and then there is a big rise in the market, the shareholder has insured that if the option is exercised, this would be his position. He would have enjoyed the $1.06 rise in price from $18.44 to $19.50. In addition, he would have enjoyed a premium of perhaps 55¢. But after the exercise of the option he would forego any further increase in the value of the shares.

Some investors may consider this a wise move on the principle that a bird in the hand is worth two in the bush. There is also the point that if the shares were to decline, in which case the option would certainly not be exercised, the premium which has been received on the sale of the option, could be considered as at least off-setting part of the decline.

Defensive action by option writers

One point to note here is that if investors who have written options against their stock believe that a large slump in share prices is imminent, such as in October 1987, it may be wise for them to put themselves in a position where they can sell their shares as a precautionary measure. As the clearing house would currently have control of the shares, one way of solving the problem is to buy a call option with the same exercise price and maturity date. The option bought and the option sold would then be closed out and the control of the shares would be passed back to the shareholder.

Using put options as an insurance against loss

Another relatively conservative use of options is to use put options as a form of insurance against market decline. Investors may consider that the market, after rising for some time, could be exposed to the possibility of a severe decline. They may hesitate to sell the shares because they feel that the present wave of enthusiasm may carry on for a while. But they need to be protected against the possibility that the enthusiasm may suddenly disappear, and the boom may become a slump.

If they buy a put option at an exercise price close to the present value of the stocks, they are protected. If a decline takes the price of the stock down by 30 per cent, they are able to exercise their right under the put option to sell the stock at the exercise price. This would then mean that they would avoid the loss. The cost to them, which is more or less the nature of an insurance premium, is the amount they pay for the put option plus transaction costs.

Further information

The subject of option trading and other uses of options is very complex. Hence, this chapter is designed simply to cover the essentials. Those seeking further information should talk to stockbrokers who are experienced in this area. They may also find it useful to read the book to which reference has already been made in this chapter, by Hugh Denning. The general information about the operation of the options market is provided in publications and educational activities arranged by the Australian Options Market. From time to time the Securities Institute of Australia also conducts lectures on this subject.

In the writing of this chapter, I have been greatly assisted by the fact that I recently attended a lecture on the subject by Michael Willis. As well as being very experienced in the options market, he also has a high degree of communication skill in explaining this matter in terms which people can readily understand. He also helped with suggestions on the working of this chapter. But it should be understood that the responsibility for the views expressed in this chapter is mine.

Futures trading

In some ways futures trading is similar to options trading in that in both areas traders are backing their judgment as to the future course of prices. But there is one very big difference. In futures trading the downside risk is open-ended.

Futures contracts generally, whether in relation to stock exchange futures or commodities, are contracts for the purchase or sale at an agreed price for delivery and settlement at an agreed later date. In the case of financial futures, such as index futures, settlement is by way of cash adjustment.

The trading in futures is far more risky than trading in options. The reason is that if the market does not co-operate with your predictions in options trading, the worst situation is that the option becomes worthless and you have lost 100 per cent of the amount you invested. But, in the futures market, if your judgments turn out to be badly incorrect, then you can lose many times the amount of the cost of the futures contract.

As markets move against you, there are margin calls which have to be paid. People who made unwise speculation in futures trading have found themselves in the same desperate position as so many people who went into negative gearing buying property, or property trusts or shares, and were severely troubled by margin calls not long afterwards.

Risk in options and futures trading

With the exception of relatively conservative uses of options to protect against a decline in the market, or to gain additional earnings from a share portfolio, this can be a very high risk area. Any form of investment in shares is a medium risk because market fluctuations can cause declines of up to 75 per cent or more in the price of very prestigious stocks, and complete recovery may take ten years. But in trading options the risk is greater because there is a risk of a loss of 100 per cent of the amount invested.

Trading in futures or options or any of the wide range of derivatives which have been developed in the past few years involves a much higher risk than the medium risk of the share investments. They all involve gearing or speculating on margins with the initial outlay on the contract being as little as 5 per cent to 10 per cent of the value of the underlying stock or index or other item on which traders back their judgment as to future market movements. This process multiplies the effect of adverse market movements so that there is a risk of loss of well over 100 per cent of invested capital.

A classic example of the extremely high risk involved was the crash, early in 1995, of the 230 year old London merchant banker, Barings Limited, apparently as the result of inadequately supervised speculative trading by a trader in Singapore.

It is obvious that trading in options and futures is not an area in which you would place next week's housekeeping money. To a considerable extent, money committed in this area should be money that you can afford to lose if fortune does not smile on you (with the exception of the more conservative uses of options, namely writing options against the shares in your portfolio, or using put options to ensure against downside risk).

Any investment in shares is a medium risk investment because periodical cyclical slumps can wipe out 40 per cent of your value, and complete recovery may take many years. Trading in options and futures trading is a high risk investment.

There is another point of which smaller investors should be aware. Even those who could prudently afford to commit some funds to options trading, should be wary of the impact of minimum brokerage charges. Minimum brokerage charges would mean a much higher effective rate of brokerage on many purchases or sales of options for one or a few contracts of 1,000 shares when the option prices are between 5¢ and 15¢.

More sophisticated uses of options

There are a number of more sophisticated uses of options which are not covered in this chapter, which is designed to help inform the typical investor with little or no experience in this area. Advice from stockbrokers who specialise in options and reference to books such as Hugh Denning's book referred to earlier could be helpful.

Chapter 20

Negative Gearing, International Stocks, Convertible Notes and Preference Shares

A cynic has said that the way to make millions in real estate is not to buy real estate but to write a book telling other people how they can make millions in real estate. In relation to negative gearing in stock investments (and indeed property) it could be said that the sure way to make very good money is to advise other people to go into gearing investments rather than to go into it yourself.

Investment advisers who recommend negative gearing into equity trusts can earn commissions of up to 16 per cent to 24 per cent or more of the investor's capital. Stockbrokers who recommend gearing investment for direct investment in shares also multiply their income considerably.

The facts and fallacies about negative gearing

As most readers would be aware, negative gearing is the term used to describe a process in which a substantial part of the cost of the investment is borrowed. The interest on the borrowed funds may exceed the net income earned by the asset, (i.e. for the present purposes shares). That loss is offset against assessable income of the investor from salary, business or professional income.

It is generally investors in the highest tax bracket who are interested in geared investing. For them the tax benefit of the deduction of the interest and the fact that capital gain on the investment is not taxed until it is realised, and then only on a portion of the gain, is naturally greater than for those with a lower marginal tax rate.

◆ *The essence of negative gearing*

Quite apart from the tax benefits in successful negative gearing operations, the basis of the approach is that it produces a multiplying effect. People with $50,000 available for investment, without gearing investing, can enjoy, if they are successful, the rate of capital gain on the purchase of an investment of $50,000.

But if they were to borrow $150,000 and invest $200,000, then the capital gain is multiplied by four. Deducting from that gain the capital gains tax payable and the net interest cost, after tax, the net result is very much greater than could have been achieved on investing only the amount of available capital, namely $50,000.

◆ *Multiplication works both ways*

The gearing which multiplies profits also multiplies losses if the market does not co-operate with the hopes of the investor. Because the total amount invested, including borrowed funds, is four times the investor's capital, then a decline in value of the investment of 20 per cent or 30 per cent, or whatever, is a loss to the investor of four times as much, i.e. 80 per cent or 120 per cent. To that loss would be added the net operating loss, i.e. the after-tax excess of interest cost over net investment income.

◆ *Range of results*

Many people have done well out of negative gearing in shares as well as property and other items. In favourable conditions the results can be very much higher than could be achieved by most other approaches to investment. But the risk is inevitably much greater.

Negative gearing is a high risk investment because there is a risk of losing well over 100 per cent of invested capital.

◆ *Favourable and unfavourable conditions*

The conditions that are favourable for gearing investing in shares include the following:

> Share values growing at a high rate in the medium to long term

> Relatively low risk of very large and/or prolonged slumps

> Relatively small difference between the after-tax income earned by the asset — in this case shares — and the after-tax interest cost.

◆ *Impact of margin calls*

Many gearing investing loan arrangements include provisions for margin calls. If the market value of the asset declines below a certain figure the investors, who are the borrowers, can be called on to "top up" the security by providing cash or acceptable securities to the lender.

If these margin calls cannot be met the effect is drastic. The principal amount of the loan which would normally have been repayable some years hence becomes payable immediately. If the investors are unable to pay the loan then they are in effect "sold up".

This deprives them of the opportunity of continuing to hold the stocks in the hope that ultimately they may recover in value. It can also leave them with a considerable liability to the lender and with the assets financed by the loan already sold.

◆ *Summary*

Any people considering negative gearing should weigh up the grandiose claims made by those who are recommending this type of investment against the facts outlined above. In good conditions gearing investing can be very rewarding. But in poor conditions it can be very adverse, even disastrous.

People going into negative gearing should ensure that, if the shares do not perform as expected, or if the income is lower than expected, they have funds available from income or other sources which can be used to avoid the disastrous effects of inability to meet margin calls and subsequent loss of the asset.

Another factor that needs to be very carefully considered is that negative gearing multiplies the charges involved. For example, for a person who invests his own capital, the capital costs of getting into and out of a unit trust can total up to six per cent or more, including some costs which may not be apparent from a quick reading of the prospectus.

If the gearing ratio is four, i.e. total investment is four times the amount of the investor's capital with the balance borrowed, the costs would be four times as great — up to 24 per cent of the investor's capital. That would mean that if the values of the underlying stocks remains steady, over a period, with no gain and no loss, geared investors would face a loss of 24 per cent of their capital.

In negative gearing for direct investment in stocks where buying and selling brokerage is much lower than brokerage on some unit trusts, the impact of costs would be considerably lower. But there would still be the effect of the costs being multiplied by the gearing.

International stocks

The advantages of investing some capital in overseas shares can be summarised as under:

> **Different risk characteristics** — Investing in international stocks in countries with economies which are basically different from Australia should reduce investment risk.

> **Favourable currency developments** — At times when the Australian dollar is weak against overseas currencies, investment overseas provides an additional gain from currency movements as well as any gain that may be achieved in the international share market.

The disadvantages of investing in overseas shares can be summarised as under:

> **Dual risk** — If currencies move the wrong way then the investor is exposed to a currency loss in addition to any loss that may occur in the overseas market. In theory, the risk of adverse movements in currency values can be minimised by placing international investments in a number of different countries, so that an adverse currency movement in one country may be offset by a favourable movement in another. In practice, it may not work out that way, because there have been times when the Australian dollar has

moved up or down in relation to several other countries at the same time.

➤ **The tendency for markets to move in tandem** — The traditional argument for some international investment to secure the benefits of international diversification has been weakened recently. Major movements in the US market have often been accompanied by somewhat similar movements in Australian and other markets — perhaps because improved communications, and freer flows of funds between countries may be leading to a "global village" for stock markets.

➤ **Limited knowledge and lower standards** — Many Australian investors are not familiar with overseas markets and overseas economies. Though that factor may be limited to some extent by the use of unit trusts which invest internationally, it is important to remember the point made earlier in the text about the inability of most unit trusts in the long term to do any better than the market average.

➤ **Different characteristics of share markets** — In some overseas countries the behaviour of the share market may be different because it may be affected by government intervention, as in Japan.

◆ *Summary*

Obviously overseas investments, whether direct investment in shares or through a unit trust, have to be considered a high risk investment, mainly because of the dual risk of currency fluctuations and market movements. While there can be a place for these investments in a portfolio, the higher risk is a good reason for the capital committed to this area to be a relatively small portion of total capital.

Unit trust investing overseas

For those investors who decide, after considering the risks in relation to their investment policy and assessing the current market conditions, that they wish to invest internationally, the case for investing through a unit trust, is probably stronger than for investment in unit trusts which invest in local stocks.

The fund managers should be able to overcome the problems of less readily available information more effectively than most individual investors.

Those investors choosing this avenue of investment should consider the points discussed in Chapter Five, especially in relation to charges and tax planning.

◆ *Overseas mutual funds*

An alternative to investing in Australian unit trusts or other managed funds is to invest in mutual funds. One big advantage is the much lower costs, for example the no entry or exit fee and annual charges of about 0.4 per cent of the Vanguard funds — see comments in Chapter Five, including the warning about Australian income tax on unrealised capital gains under some circumstances.

Convertible securities

Convertible securities are debt instruments, (i.e. bonds or debentures) or preference shares of a company that may be changed into a specified number of ordinary shares of the company. There is a wide variety of different types of convertible securities. The comments below are subject to the effect of the provisions in the terms of issue.

◆ *Advantages*

The main advantages of convertible securities are as under:

➢ **Higher yield** — The investor obtains the right to become the owner of shares at a future date at a yield which is generally much higher than the yield on a purchase of the ordinary shares.

➢ **Lower downside risk** — The downside risk is lower than for the ordinary shares in the same company. There are two base factors which tend to underpin the value of convertible securities. One is the investment value which is an estimate of what the security would sell for if there were no conversion rights. The other is the conversion parity, i.e. the market value of the stock multiplied by the number of shares to be received on conversion for each convertible security.

♦ *Disadvantages*

The disadvantage of convertible securities are as under:

➤ **Problems with the company** — Possible decline in earnings or prospects of the company causing a decline in market value could make the conversion less attractive.

➤ **Problems in share or bond markets** — An overall stock market slump can reduce the potential conversion benefits. An overall decline in the bond market, such as that which occurred in 1994, would reduce the value of the bond as a fixed-interest investment, i.e the investment value referred to above.

♦ *Summary*

On balance, there is a case for share investors considering investing some funds in convertible securities which are, in a sense, a half-way home between fixed interest and share investments. But they would need to consider the points discussed above and be fully aware of the benefits and risks of the stock into which the securities are to be converted. The questions of overall trends, risk and timing are also relevant.

Chapter 21

How to
Avoid Common
Errors

It has been said that those who ignore history are ultimately overwhelmed by it. For many investors the problem is that lessons are not learned from the mistakes of the past. Sometimes this is not so much the fault of the investors, but of the investment business which refuses to acknowledge mistakes.

Fund managers, investment advisers and others have been wildly enthusiastic about the stock market when it is at very high levels, when history shows quite clearly that it is better to sell than to buy. When the slump commences soon afterwards they do not show any regret or learn from the lessons of the past. So it is very important that investors are clearly aware of a number of common mistakes and how to avoid them.

The policy strategy and the portfolio effect

The error — Investors are persuaded to purchase a stock or a particular type of unit trust without adequate consideration of the implications of the purchase on the investment policy which they should be following, a strategy based on timing, the position of the market and the effect on their overall portfolio.

How to avoid — The fact that a particular stock or a type of unit trust has intrinsic merits is not, in itself, enough to justify a decision to buy. You would need to consider whether the proposed purchase would bring total equity investments above the maximum in policy limit for your particular situation, or whether a possibly much smaller percentage of your total capital is warranted under present conditions from the viewpoint of prices being at a dangerously high level. The above indicators are discussed in Chapter Thirteen and the zones from high to low which are discussed in other chapters. If the proposed purchase is sufficiently attractive the wise course may be, if necessary, to sell one of your other stocks so that the new investment would fit in with the above standards.

Making decisions based on market fables, fallacies and folklore

The error — Many people do not do well with shares because so much investment material states, or strongly implies, that "good" shares — including the market leaders in the so called blue chips — are a safe haven in difficult times because they are immune from slumps or that if companies continue to report good earnings growth it must be reflected in increased share prices.

How to avoid — Remember that leading stocks are not immune to market slumps and sometimes the decline in value of those stocks is more severe and more prolonged than in other stocks. Growth in earnings may have been anticipated, or over-anticipated, to produce unrealistically high share prices. The result could be that even if the expected growth in earnings is realised the price of the stock may decline rather than rise.

It is also necessary to take into account the question of whether the overall market is at dangerously high levels and the impact of all psychological factors discussed in Chapter Eighteen.

The reality is that from the viewpoint of influences on results, the purchase of shares or equity trusts is not solely an investment in a company but in an unstable and unpredictable market. What happens in the market, including psychological factors and reaction to previous excessive booms, can have a greater effect on the result of the investment than the fortunes of the company.

Failure to make precautionary sales before a slump

The error — Investors are persuaded by fund managers or advisers not to make partial sales of their holdings to protect the capital from the erosion in a slump which appears to be imminent. The advice not to sell is often supported by false claims that timing does not matter, that in this particular boom price rises will continue because "things are different this time". The increase may be based on the efficient market hypothesis that the price of a particular stock at any time represents the best estimate of what it should be.

How to avoid — Use the principles discussed in this book to make investment decisions on the basis of medium term timing. Remember the wisdom of three old sayings, namely, nobody ever went broke taking a profit, a profit is not a profit until it is in the bank and eager sellers make good investors.

Making buying or selling decisions on the basis of superficial conventional analysis

The error — Most of the comments and recommendations about ordinary shares and unit trusts, as well as media discussion, relates to earnings per share and price earning multiples. Moreover, many fund managers and other institutions buy stocks at unsustainably high prices and fail to sell before there is trouble. So it is not surprising that results of many individual investors are disappointing because they rely unduly on this conventional superficial analysis.

How to avoid — They need to go beyond the conventional approach at least into a study of the trend in return on equity in making their estimates as to future growth in earnings per share and impact on share prices. It is desirable that they should go one stage further into the analysis of the components of earnings which was discussed in Chapter Seventeen.

Placing undue emphasis on taxation or means test considerations

The error — Disappointing results and sometimes serious losses have occurred because investors place too much emphasis on the tax or Means Test benefits of certain heavily promoted investments.

How to avoid — Investors must be constantly on their guard against having the taxation tail wag the sound investment dog. It is a lot better to share a profit with the tax people or receive a slightly lower pension, than to have a big loss later on. Do your investment and financial planning on an after-tax basis, but assess investments firstly on the basis of their commercial soundness. If one commercially sound investment offers a tax benefit then that could make it preferable to others.

But do not let taxation benefits be the sole or primary standard of assessment. The schemes put forward as great tax savers generally involve a significantly higher risk which would not be appropriate for most investors.

An unrealistic approach to selling

The error — Many investors make the mistake of not converting the maybe money of unrealised capital gain into the actual money of realised gains or fail to cut their losses by selling at a loss in the early stage of the slump rather than facing a bigger loss later on. Disappointments arise because of the decision to sell only if a stock reaches a certain price, but its rising trend stops a little short of that price and then declines significantly.

Some investors accept the false claim that when the value of a share declines you have not made a loss unless you sell it. The reality is that a loss has occurred. Failing to sell at least part of your holding does not affect the reality of the decline. The problem with investors who defer selling action is that they delude themselves that they would not know what to do with the money if they sold the shares.

How to avoid — If you are not prepared to face up to selling decisions you should not invest in shares. Many people find it difficult to make selling decisions when they are warranted. As timing is so important in share results, they must develop the mental discipline to make selling decisions. Failure to make sales when warranted often means the difference between a good resale and an average or sometimes below average resale. Postponing sales in the hope of ultimate recovery may involve a significant opportunity cost if recovery takes many years. As to what to do with the funds after you sell, there are always alternative opportunities — whether they be in fixed-interest investments for a while if the overall market is in a slump, or is likely to go into a slump fairly soon, or to switch into other shares or other types of unit trusts under current conditions.

Signing a blank cheque by way of dividend reinvestment

The error — For many investors, when the stock market goes into a decline or a particular stock or unit trust which has been doing very well declines, the inevitable reaction to such abnormal rises is much greater because investors have been regularly placing more money in that stock by way of dividend reinvestment.

How to avoid — Though dividend reinvestment appeals to many investors, it is not sound because of the important fact that stock market investing calls for two requirements — finding a stock with attractive features and future prospects and buying it at a price which is attractive in relation to dividend yield and earnings compared with other stocks or other investments. Investors would not agree to a suggestion from a broker or anyone else to buy shares in a certain company in six months time or three years time or five years time at an unknown price and at an unknown dividend yield. But that process of giving a blank cheque is involved in dividend reinvestment schemes.

The ability to buy shares without paying brokerage and often at a moderate discount to market value is a plus factor that is not sufficient to offset that intrinsic weakness of this concept. Consider also the significantly higher accounting costs incurred in calculating the indexed cost base for capital gains tax when stocks are sold.

Disappointing results through dollar cost averaging

The error — Making further investment in a stock in which prices have declined since original purchase in order to achieve a lower average cost. If the stock recovers quickly then rises rapidly that process may work but very often the opposite is the result.

How to avoid — In deciding whether to increase your holding of a certain stock, the price at which you purchased your present holding is not a relevant consideration. The decision should be made on assessment of the present situation and future prospects of the stock in relation to earnings and other matters. The current situation and likely trends of the stock market as discussed in Chapter Thirteen and the zone system of ranking discussed in earlier chapters are relevant in this regard. There could be times when such an assessment would suggest further investment in the stock. If so a decision to buy may be wise — subject to consideration of the effect on the overall portfolio. It would also be necessary to consider the investment in that industry and policy and strategy considerations referred to above and in earlier chapters. But the decision to buy should never be based simply on the result that the average price per share would be reduced.

Ineffective management of portfolio

The error — Disappointing investment results may arise because of ineffective management of the overall portfolio. For example, there may be so many stocks in the portfolio that overall management is impaired because the investor gives insufficient attention to monitoring them closely. Reviewing on the basis of yield related to cost price rather than to yield at the current market price is another example. Setting unrealistic buying and selling limits on orders or sticking to a good thing for too long or falling in love with your stocks are other management errors.

How to avoid — Consolidate your portfolio to a limited number of stocks which is big enough to give adequate diversification and not too big for effective management. This generally means somewhere between about six to ten stocks for the average individual portfolio. If you have decided that a stock should be bought or sold then do not run the risk of missing out on opportunities by setting unrealistic limits on your orders. Your high regard for a company or your appreciation of the profit you have earned from a stock in the past is not, of itself, a good enough reason to continue holding a stock when an objective assessment would indicate that at least a partial sale is warranted.

Insufficient attention to risk

The error — Failing to give adequate attention to the full extent of risk involved in share investments causes disappointing results. This is not surprising because the fast growing business of risk concealing means that investors do not have adequate information on this question.

How to avoid — In making investment decisions, be aware of the various risks involved including information or accounting risk, i.e. the risk of loss because figures in the financial statements or other information may not be reliable. Beware of buying or continuing to hold shares in a company in which the borrowings are unduly high. Remember the importance of market risk, the possibility of the loss of 40 per cent of capital or more in a market slump with many years to recovery, and the fact that there have been periods of up to 15 years in which the stock market has failed to provide any sustained net gain. Remember too that spreading your capital over a number of different stocks does not provide any real protection against market risk which is often the most significant risk.

Chapter 22

A Summary
of Realistic
Investing

An old style country preacher instructing an assistant said, "First you tells 'em what yo're goin to tell 'em, then you tells them, then you tells 'em what you just told 'em". So this chapter summarises the contents of the book in the form of the following 12 basic principles on which realistic investing is based.

♦ *Knowledge*

1. Know the significance of the real components of return
2. Understand the real nature of the stock market
3. Know the dimensions of stock market movements

♦ *Fundamental*

4. Never forget the crucial importance of medium term timing
5. Base all decisions on a suitable policy and timely strategy
6. Recognise all types of risk and beware of risk concealers
7. Develop a capacity for making selling decisions
8. Allow for psychological factors, e.g. the herd instinct
9. Differentiate between fact and fallacy on unit trusts

♦ *Operational*

10. Concentrate on less well known and less popular stocks
11. Analyse to find the right stock at the right price
12. Maintain a well spread but compact portfolio.

As a reminder of the detailed comments throughout the book, set out below are brief comments on each of these 12 principles.

Know the impact of the four components of return

There are four components in return on share investments, namely the initial dividend yield, increase in dividend during the period the investment is held, the tax credit on some dividends and increase due to change in price dividend multiple between purchase and sale date. The portion of earnings which is not distributed is not a component of total return. Expectations that undistributed earnings will be reflected in enhanced prices do not always eventuate.

◆ *Initial Dividend yield*

Nearly always the initial dividend yield has a big effect on overall return. History shows that, generally, investing on a relatively high dividend yield, i.e. when prices are in Zones 4 or 5 (as discussed in Chapter One), produces good results with low downside risk and vice versa for investing when prices are in Zones 2 or 1.

It is important to remember that it is changes in the direction and extent of movements in share prices which are the main cause of the difference between extremely good and extremely bad results.

Understand the real nature of the stock market

The share market for much of the time is volatile and unstable. The reality includes frantic booms followed by severe reactions which have been characteristics of markets at least since the South Sea Bubble 250 years ago. That contrasts with the picture of an efficient market based on rational decisions portrayed by the efficient market hypothesis and capital asset pricing model. The pervasive influence of risk concealers is a big factor.

Know the dimensions of the stock market

The dimensions of the share market could be summarised as under:

➤ **Long term** — Results are generally better than other investments.

➤ **Average capital gain** — Over the long term, capital gain averages about 6.5 per cent per annum compound.

➤ **Variation** — There is a very wide range above and below that average. Even over periods as long as five years, the change in share prices has ranged from a gain of about 330 per cent to a loss of about 55 per cent of capital.

➤ **Absence of sustained gain** — There have been periods of up to 15 years in which there has been no net sustained gain in the All Ordinaries Index.

➤ **Dividend growth** — Long term dividend growth tends to average about 6 per cent per annum compound, i.e. it would double in about 12 years but the rate of growth is variable.

Never forget the importance of medium term timing

Financial fables, fallacies and folklore, plus strenuous efforts by many fund managers and risk concealers have misled many people into thinking that timing does not matter. This is obviously untrue. The five year capital gain of those who invested in shares in 1982, before the boom, was vastly better than for those who invested in September 1987 just before the crash.

It is futile to try to pick the precise bottom or top of market cycles because it is still true that nobody rings a bell at those points. But medium term timing, using the principles discussed in this book, is a practicable approach. Even moderate success can produce far better results than just drifting up and down with the market tide.

◆ *Step system*

Remember it is not a matter of making one decision to be wholly in or wholly out of the market. By buying or selling some shares initially, and then watching the market closely for decisions on future purchases or sales, it is possible to fine tune the decisions on the basis of more up-to-date information.

Base decisions on a suitable policy and timely strategy

All investors need to have a policy appropriate to their situation based on their age, income from other sources, likely needs for large amounts of cash in the next few years, attitude to risk-taking and taxation situation. The policy would normally be set on a semi-permanent basis. It would be changed only when there were significant changes in those basic factors.

But because the timing is so important and conditions in share markets are constantly changing, there is a need for a strategy which depends on timing considerations. For example, if the policy decision were to have somewhere between zero and 40 per cent in the stock market, then at times when objective indications are that share prices may be dangerously high, the percentage in the share market would be gradually reduced towards the lower end of that range and vice versa.

Be aware of all types of risk and the risk concealers

> **Volatility not best measure** — The capital asset pricing model assumption that risk can be measured by volatility, i.e. standard deviation, is not sound. What investors need to know is not the extent to which returns vary over short to medium periods, but the maximum loss over a reasonable time horizon, e.g. five years.

> **Main risk overlooked** — Most investment theory and much investment practice overlooks the most important risk, namely risk due to market fluctuations as distinct from risk due to changing fortunes of a company. Moreover, company risk can be minimised by a spread of investment, but that is no help for market risk.

> **Accounting information risk** — Another important risk is the possibility of loss through audited financial statements portraying a situation which differs a great deal from reality and that the information available from various sources in the investment world is incorrect because it has been affected by the operations of the risk concealers.

> **Medium or high risk** — Shares, like any other market investments, are normally a medium risk, but when a boom pushes prices to very high levels this can change them into high risk.

> **High risk through borrowing** — Share investments can also change to a high risk if they involve borrowing, including negative gearing.

Allow for psychological factors e.g. the herd instinct

The rate of change in share prices and even the direction of the movement, for some periods, may differ from what a rational objective analysis would suggest. The market is not immune to fads and fashions, irrational decisions, mob psychology and the herd instinct which affect events in other areas.

By being aware of those influences which are now receiving more attention from behavioural finance people, investors may be able to improve their returns in good times and protect their capital from erosion by precautionary sales before the hysteria of the boom turns in to the despondency of the slump that inevitably follows a boom.

Separate fact from fallacy on unit trusts and managed funds

Remember that much of the rhetoric in prospectuses and comments of investment advisers and in the financial press about managed funds is not borne out by the facts. Experience shows that most managers fail to do as well as the market average. Costs and charges are one of the reasons for that situation.

In equity trusts, particularly at times of low dividend yields, the costs can be very significant, with management charges and expenses absorbing up to 90 per cent of the dividend income.

In some cases there could be merit in considering investment in low cost unit trusts or low cost US mutual funds.

Develop a capacity for making selling decisions

Because of the importance of timing and the need to keep risk to tolerable levels, investors need to develop a capacity to make selling decisions.

Three old sayings should be remembered — "Nobody ever went broke taking a profit", "a profit is not a profit until it is in the bank" and "eager sellers make good investors".

♦ *Selling time for every stock*

Sooner or later every stock, including those which have had spectacularly good performances, become better selling than buying.

♦ *Step system in selling (and also in buying)*

Remember that one of the advantages of shares is that you can use the step system by selling part of the holding immediately and then watching the market closely for any further selling.

Concentrate on less well known and less popular stocks

Well known and popular stocks tend to be generally overpriced because there are so many analysts and financial writers following them. Often when a stock reaches the stage of being in most institutional portfolios and being followed by a number of security analysts, then, even though it may continue to perform well in the future, its better days are behind it. Well selected stocks with small capital have produced better results than the leaders.

Analysis must find the right stock at the right price

It is not enough for analysis to find "good" stocks in a promising industry with good earnings records and prospects and a strong financial position. What you must seek are stocks which are good value *at current price*.

♦ *Cost price and yield on cost price not relevant*

In reviewing a portfolio or an individual stock, the cost price of the stock, or the yield based on the cost price, is not really relevant. What must be considered are the present position and future prospects of the stock, on the basis of the current price dividend multiple or dividend yield as well as current and expected growth in earnings and dividends.

♦ *Overall market effect*

As movements in the overall market generally form a significant part of the results of an investment in a particular stock, this should be a paramount factor in considerations.

♦ *Overall portfolio effect*

Remember that review, and all investment decisions, must be made in terms of the overall portfolio effect and not in isolation.

♦ *Avoid reinvestment schemes*

Decisions to reinvest dividends are in effect decisions to buy a pig in a poke. They authorise the investment of additional capital in a company at unknown prices, and unknown prospects sometime in the future.

♦ *Avoid averaging down*

Never increase your holdings of shares when prices have decreased just to produce a lower average cost. Whether it is wise to invest more funds in a company because the share prices have declined is a matter of considering all the relevant factors, including overall market situation and the relative attractions of that stock compared with others.

Maintain a well spread but compact portfolio

Portfolios should be spread over enough stocks to reduce risk but be limited to a number which makes the task of management more practicable. For individual investors, somewhere between six and twelve stocks would be appropriate. Remember the point made earlier that, however widely a portfolio is spread, that is no protection against what is generally the biggest risk of all, namely the risk of market decline.

♦ *Be open to buy*

Wise investors generally do not put the whole of the capital, which they have decided could be invested in the share market, into shares immediately. It is often wise to keep a portion of capital, perhaps 10 per cent or so, in reserve to take advantage of any special situations that may arise, including attractive new issues.

Appendix A

How to Find
Information
and Access its
Reliability

The nature of the problem

It has been said that in war, truth is the first casualty. The same comment is substantially true in relation to the investment business because a large part of the available information is not true.

The point was made in Chapter One about untrue, inaccurate or misleading information provided by those who make a lot of money through the large and growing investment business of risk concealing. The desire to earn brokerage, or management fees or commissions encourages many people in the business to convey information that is untrue. Often, the problem is that it is a half truth which it has been said is more dangerous than a lie, just as a half brick can be more dangerous than a full brick because you can throw it further and more accurately.

Sometimes the untrue or inaccurate information that clients receive is not necessarily due to a callous disregard of the truth by investment people but the "Goebbeling" process leads to it being accepted as true.

Extent of the problem

In case you think that the above comments may be a little extreme ask yourself about these significant information areas:

➢ **Nature of share market** — How many recommendations for share investments which you have seen, pointed out the risk factors which were discussed in Chapter One? A major risk factor is that even over five years, capital gain can vary from a massive gain of over 330 per cent to a loss of over 57 per cent. Another is that there have been periods of up to 15 years in which the share market has produced no sustained and net gain.

➤ **Prospectuses** — How many prospectuses or annual reports or other publications of unit trust companies have disclosed the above information?

➤ **Media comments** — How many articles in the financial press and in financial magazines, or contributors to radio and TV programs have disclosed any of the above facts?

➤ **Books** — How many books on investment have given a clear indication of the above and other realities which are discussed in this book?

➤ **Educational courses** — How many courses at educational institutions have been so concentrated on what happens to be the popular theory at the time, such as the efficient market hypothesis over the last 20 or 30 years, that they failed to inform students of the realities of the stock market referred to above?

➤ **Imminent slumps** — How many of the above sources warned in October 1987, or at the end of 1993, that despite prospects from an improving economy stock prices were at dangerously high levels? Or that on the basis of past experience, at those levels, prospects for good gain were limited and downside risk was increased?

➤ **Protection of investors' capital** — How many of the fund managers whose alleged expertise in investment management is so heavily promoted took at least some defensive action by precautionary sales, the use of options or any other method to preserve their clients' capital from the erosion in slumps which then appeared to be likely?

What investors need to do

In this situation it is not simply a matter of investors knowing where to look for information about investment matters. They need to be aware of any possible bias, often a subconscious and innocent bias in information so that they can make an assessment of how reliable it may be.

A first step for the typical investor is to make use of the facilities which are available to them through non-profit organisations which are not subject to the temptations of commercial organisations which often result in information from those latter sources being less than objective.

The Australian Investors Association (AIA)

This is a non-profit organisation which I founded in 1992. Its objectives, in brief, are to achieve a fair go for investors of every kind including shareholders, investors in unit trusts, debentures, bank deposits, superannuation funds, rollover funds, allocated pensions, friendly societies, investment bonds, and life insurance.

One of its specific objectives is to persuade the Federal Government that all people who offer their services as investment advisers meet three basic standards — namely, that they operate on a genuine professional basis of charging a time-based fee with any commissions received being passed on to the client, that they have tertiary qualifications in accounting, commerce or an allied field and that they have had adequate real investment experience as distinct from marketing investment products.

Its activities include the issue of *Investor Alerts* to warn investors of traps for the unwary in certain types of investments, an area in which generally available information is inaccurate, inadequate or misleading.

It was one of these *Alerts* which I wrote, issued in November 1993, three months before the 1994 market slump commenced, that on objective grounds, share prices were at dangerously high levels and a slump was a distinct possibility. It also pointed out that all or most of the predictions that share prices would continue to rise were from sources which had a vested interest in talking up the market while those who could be more objective were considerably more cautious.

The AIA maintains a list of investment advisers who meet the standards set out above and who also give certain undertakings to fully disclose all material information about the full extent of investment risk.

The contact address for information about the AIA is Box 5 Post Office Graceville East, Qld 4075, Phone 07 892 4848 Fax 07 892 3744.

Australian Shareholders Association (ASA)

This non-profit association was established in 1968. It is well known for its efforts in many fields related to the share market, shareholders and listed companies. One of its more recent achievements was the production jointly with the Australian Institute of Company Directors of a publication entitled *The Conduct of Annual General Meetings — Code of Best Practice*.

For many years, ASA representatives have spoken out at company meetings whenever there have been matters of concern to public shareholders.

In the field of financial statements, the ASA has been active both in making representations to government on the need for improvements and in raising queries at annual general meetings when warranted.

Seeing that the interests of minority shareholders are protected in takeovers is another matter on which the ASA has been active.

A quarterly publication *Equity* is published by the ASA. A recent issue contained articles on stapled securities, an assessment into the ASC report into the Girvan Corporation, a comment on the NRMA prospectus and the later Court action, and details of matters of concern to the ASA at annual general meetings of 12 different listed companies. There was also an announcement that the ASA had negotiated with a broking firm an arrangement for that firm to conduct broking business for ASA members at a very attractive rate.

The contact address for the Australian Shareholders Association is GPO Box 5210 Sydney NSW 2001, Phone (02) 282 6982 Fax (02) 212 5636.

Co-operation between the AIA and ASA

For some time the AIA and ASA have been working closely together with invitations to members of each body to attend educational meetings of the other body. The Councils of both organisations look forward to progressing to even closer co-operation in future in seeking the common goal of a better deal for investors.

The American Association of Independent Investors

Naturally this US non-profit association has a membership base and financial resources that are many times as great as the Australian organisations. Some Australian investors may wish to join the US organisation to enjoy their journal and other benefits described below. Even if you are not very interested in investing in US stocks, the various information services of this association would be valuable because they also cover investment principles and practices, most of which are of interest to Australian as well as US investors.

Annual subscription is $US49 or about AUS67 at the current exchange rate at the end of February 1995.

◆ *AAII Journal*

The Journal is published ten times a year, monthly, except for March and December. Each issue of this publication contains interesting, stimulating and practical articles, on a wide range of topical matters. Most of them contain information which is not available elsewhere. Because of the non-profit nature of the organisation, the material is considerably more factual and objective than in many other popular publications.

◆ *Computerised investment bulletin*

AAII members have the option of subscribing to the bulletin, *Computerized Investing* for the additional subscription of $US19. It is issued bi-monthly and contains a wide range of articles on the use of computers in investing including the AAII On Line details of products for use in mutual funds and common stocks screening and other topics of interest to those who use computers to help them in investments.

◆ *Low load mutual funds*

For an additional subscription of $US19, AAII members can receive the *Individual Investor's Guide to Low Load Mutual Funds* which is mailed in March of each year. It provides information in relation to over 800 no-load and low-load mutual funds including one, three, five and ten year annual return, risk measures, bull and bear market performance, beta for stock funds, average maturity for bond funds, portfolio turnover, expense ratios, distributors and net asset value.

The address of the American Association of Individual Investors is 625 North Michigan Avenue, Chicago, Illinois 60611 - 3110 phone (312) 280 8170 fax (312) 280 1625.

Other sources of information and advice

◆ *Stockbrokers*

Stockbroking firms usually provide to clients, information and advice on individual stocks and their assessment of prospects for industries and for the overall market. Reviews of companies and estimates of company earnings and dividends by most broking firms are generally of a high quality.

As an indication of the type of material which is available from some firms, set out below is a selection of recent publications of a major stockbroking firm:

➢ The February issue of *Investment Review* which contained an article on "Looking for yield" including three reviews of stocks offering high yields, recommendations of two international equity investments, an explanation of the new Stock Exchange Clearing House Electronic Sub register System (CHESS), details of two of the firm's new unit trusts and an article on transitional arrangements in relation to the new reasonable benefit limits for superannuation.

➢ The stockbroking firm's *Stock Book* with brief comments, "investment arithmetic" and brief reviews of about 100 stocks in 20 different industry categories, together with sector outlooks for each industry grouping, as well as reviews of the relative performance of recommended equity portfolios to meet different objectives and analysts' forecasts of key items — namely, net profit growth, earnings per share growth, dividend per share growth, nominal dividend yield and percentage franked, for the industrial sector, excluding banks and property trusts, resource sector and resource sector excluding BHP.

➢ Company reporting calendar and results forecasts for 110 leading industrial companies.

➤ Industry reviews for the transport and media sectors

➤ *The Australian Economic Monitor*, a 64 page publication which includes comment, figures and charts and forecasts of many key economic indicators.

Combining broker comments with other sources

With due respect to the broking publications, most of them tend to be based mainly on the traditional investment approach with a fairly heavy emphasis on leading stocks and the so called blue chips. In my view, it is desirable to consider that type of comment in conjunction with comments from other sources.

Newsletters

There are a number of newsletters of various types which cover share market investing.

Donnelly's Investing Today, which I founded many years ago and of which I am the editor, is published by Donnelly Money Management Pty. Ltd.

Newton's Global Economic Report. This report concentrates on the big picture, on long term trends which operate over periods of five years or more. It does this to help subscribers identify major movements and to stick with them.

Ian Huntley Pty. Ltd. Newsletters. This company publishes two newsletters, *Your Money Weekly* deals largely with leading stocks and the better second-liners. *Penny Share Guide* deals with what the conventional investment wisdom describes as speculative stocks, namely, mineral exploration stocks.

Information about listed companies

A useful publication is *The Australian Financial Review Shareholder — The Handbook of Australian Public Companies* which is issued each six months. It contains detailed information on the 500 largest listed companies which is a large portion of the total number of listed companies.

Each page contains a great deal of information about each company. There is a chart of the share price for the last ten years which also included the All Ordinaries Index and the consumer price index. Financial data for the last five years includes profit figures and dividends, as well as key balance sheet data. Other investment indicators for the last five years which are included are earnings per share — historical and adjusted — dividends per share, percentage of dividend franked, net tangible asset value per share — historical and adjusted — and high and low share prices.

There is a summary of the nature of the business conducted by each company, details of directors, senior management and auditors, capital structure, substantial shareholdings, and top 20 holders of ordinary shares. There is also a brief summary of events in the reporting period.

The publication also includes a number of articles about industry segments. It is available from Stafford McWilliams Pty. Ltd. Phone (02) 975 1705 or fax (02) 975 3801. As at March 1995 the price is $44.95 plus postage and packing of $5.00.

Some of the above types of information about a smaller group of listed companies can be found in the *All Ordinaries Index Companies Handbook* published by Australian Stock Exchange.

Other publications

My book *More Wealth Through Beating the Money Traps — A Survival Guide to Today's Investing Jungle* covers traps for the unwary and how to overcome the serious information deficiencies in prospectuses, advertisements reports and comments of many fund managers, advisers and other investment sources.

Of particular interest to share investors are chapters on how individual investors can achieve results through company meetings.

The book includes two successful David and Goliath stories, in which I was involved, of success by minority groups against the odds. This book is priced at $20.00 plus $3.00 posting and packing. See the request for services form at the end of this book.

The statistical department of Australian Stock Exchange publishes a loose-leaf service of reviews of all listed companies which include, as well as summaries of announcements to the Exchange, summaries of profit and loss accounts and balance sheets for 10 years. This service is not cheap, but most brokers allow clients to study this material if they wish to do so.

The *AXJ Journal* which is published by Australian Stock Exchange comes with the monthly *Personal Investment* to subscribers (but not to buyers of *Personal Investment* from newsagents). It contains, as well as articles on investment matters, details of share prices, and volume for the month and year to date. Another section of the journal includes current profit figures, earnings per share, dividend yield, debt to equity ratio and price to net asset ratio for all listed stocks.

The *Australian Financial Review* and the business pages of the national newspaper, *The Australian,* contain prices of shares and options as well as dividend yields and other information as well as articles on investment matters. The business pages of metropolitan daily newspapers also contain details on listed companies.

Particularly useful is the list of the 150 largest listed companies which is published each Monday in the *Sydney Morning Herald*. That list includes the important indicator — namely, return on equity — on shareholders' funds as well as the grossed up dividend yield, i.e. the dividend yield adjusted for the applicable tax credit.

Educational Activities

There are many seminars, etc. on investments which are described as educational. But many of them are sales campaigns thinly disguised as education. It would be fair comment to state that most of such activities which are offered free or for a nominal charge would be in the sales promotion category rather than real education.

Investment advisers and financial planners

Analysis of the merits of the very large number of people which the inefficient regulation system allows to conduct business as investment advisers in Australia is a little like the biblical story of finding five just men. The position can be summarised as under:

Sellers of investments — The majority of them derive their income entirely or mainly from commissions. That includes many who include a small or almost nominal fee component in their basis of remuneration in the hope of appearing to be professional. So despite the claims they make those advisers are not independent. Some large accounting firms claim to be objective and operate on a fee basis. But, in fact, they work on a disguised commission basis by the process of charging so called lodgement fees of up to 3.5 per cent of amount invested which means that the bulk of the commission stays with them.

Massive losses — The fact that so many of the so called advisers are really sales people masquerading as advisers is a major reason for investors suffering very large losses in equity trusts and other investments due to the failure of the "advisers" to disclose all material information especially the full extent of the risk involved.

Qualifications and experience — The majority are without tertiary qualifications in accounting, commerce, or allied fields which are necessary for proper analysis of investments. Most also lack adequate real investment experience as distinct from experience in selling investment products.

Genuine professional advisers — Only a handful of advisers are on the Practitioner Members list of the Australian Investors Association. That list comprises people who, being members of the Association, support its objectives and are also advisers who meet the AIA standards referred to above in relation to operating on a genuine professional fee basis with qualifications and experience.

They also give certain undertakings concerning disclosing all material information including the full extent of the risk involved. Another undertaking is that recommendations of shares or share-based investments will not include any estimate of future capital gain. The reason for the AIA requiring that undertaking is that the reality of such very wide variations (from a 330 per cent gain to a loss of 57 per cent over five years) means that any estimate would be meaningless and could be misleading.

A copy of the AIA Practitioner Members List can be obtained on request, accompanied by a stamped addressed envelope, from the AIA, Box 5 Post Office, Graceville East, Queensland 4075.

Matters to consider in using information and advice

In considering how the information and advice available from various sources should be used, it is vital that you remember the points made at the beginning of this Appendix and elsewhere throughout the book that a great deal — possibly the majority — of investment information is unreliable and may be dangerously misleading.

Specifically you should remember these points:

➤ **Timing** — There is no truth in the widely publicised claim, which is the basis for a lot of advice and information that it is always a good time to buy shares.

➤ **The time for buying** — The reality is that because of the wide variation in stock price movements, decisions to buy and sell shares should be based on a recognition of the need to increase investments when the market is in Zones 4 or 5 and reduce them when it is in Zones 1 or 2.

➤ **Market factors often crucial** — Despite good performance and prospects of a company, the shares of that company can be a poor investment if they are bought when a boom has pushed the overall market or the price of that stock up to dangerously high levels. The law of gravity has not been repealed.

➤ **Goebbeling** — Remember that the comments of highly respected investment figures and academics may be unreliable if only because they have allowed themselves to be "Goebbeled" into accepting as true an untrue statement that has been repeated for a long time.

➤ **Objective material** — Subject to the importance of timing, make maximum use of objective material that is available from non-commercial, non-profit, organisations such as the Australian Investors Association which are discussed above.

On the basis of 40 years investment experience that approach could put you well on the path to survival in today's investment information jungle.

Annex to Appendix A

Copy of page 3
of February 1995 issue of
Donnelly's Investing Today

Income and possible capital gain or loss on shares compared with other investments

Adjusted dividend yield — In considering results over the medium term (five years), it is first necessary to adjust the average dividend yield. To allow for the tax credit which applies to about two thirds of dividends, the average dividend yield is multiplied by 1.3. Then to allow for gradual increase in dividend income, that factor should be increased to 1.5 (except when dividend growth is small or negative).

Capital gain in past — Our database shows that over the last 30 years the average capital gain before tax has been in the 5 per cent to 6.5 per cent per annum range. In about one quarter of the periods, the result was a loss.

Yield at time of investment — Investing when average dividend yield is in Zones 4 or 5, has generally produced higher gains with lower downside risk than investing at other times.

Present income situation — With average yield of 3.9 per cent and adjustment factor 1.5 this is equal to 5.9 per cent on other investments — compared with returns of up to 10.0 per cent on low risk fixed interest.

Possible after-tax returns — If the capital gain achieved over the next five years equals the long term average, the after-tax return to a share investor in the top marginal tax bracket would be 6.8 per cent compared with 5.3 per cent on fixed-interest investments. For investors in the lowest tax bracket, i.e. 15 per cent, (e.g. super funds), the share return would be 8.6 per cent compared with 8.7 per cent on fixed-interest investments. If capital gain equals the best over

30 years the share results would be between 24.4 per cent and 34.2 per cent per annum after tax.

If they equalled the worst result there would be an after-tax loss of about 8.8 per cent to 11.4 per cent per annum compound.

Australian Shares — All Ordinaries Index — Minor Swings Omitted

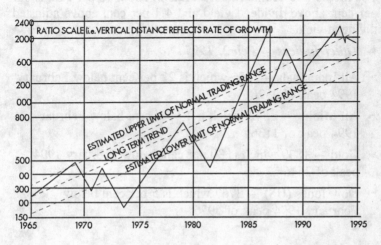

Present Position — February 2, 1995 All Ords 1857, i.e. 21 per cent below February 1994 peak of 2341.

How much blue sky? — The market continues to be approximately 23 per cent above long term trend. At that level, experience suggests greater probability of disappointing results rather than good gain.

Downside risk related to long term trend — From current position 23 per cent above long term trend, there could be a decline of 33 per cent or more if, as in the past, the market falls below the trend line before starting sustained recovery.

Current market mood — Until the slight recovery which started at the end of the first week in February, the mood had been depressed and uncertain. As the low point of 1831 late in January was about level with August 1993, the market has been off the boil with no net gain for 18 months. A strong day on Wall Street on Friday, February 3, may help for a while but the market is right now not robust.

Average dividend yield — 3.9 per cent per annum.

Adjusted yield (to reflect tax credits and expected increase in dividend income) — 5.9 per cent per annum.

◆ *Income Handicap*

The medium term fixed-interest rate of about 10 per cent is 6.1 per cent above dividend yield and 4.1 per cent above adjusted dividend yield.

◆ *Other Indices — Feb 2, 1995*

➤ All Industrials —2756 which is 22 per cent below February 1994 peak of 3526

➤ All Mining — 842 which is 19 per cent below February 1994 peak of 1136

➤ Gold — 1839 which is 30 per cent below February 1994 peak of 2646

➤ Dow Jones (US) — 3767 which is 5 per cent below February 1994 peak of 3976.

Appendix B

After-Tax
Returns

Some years ago we decided to publish in each issue of *Donnelly's Investing Today,* important information which is not available elsewhere — namely, the estimated after-tax return over the next five years for shares and fixed-interest investments for the highest marginal tax rate of 47 per cent and the lowest of 15 per cent which applies to superannuation funds. The estimate takes into account all available information, namely, the current average dividend yield, estimated increase in dividend receipts, and the tax credit. The capital gain estimate is objective, being the average five year gain achieved over 360 rolling periods of five years in our database which goes back to 1960. We also show the range, by including what the result would be if the capital gain over the next five years equalled the best and worst five year results since 1960.

Set out below is the relevant information from our February 1995 issue — the figures are per cent per annum compound.

♦ *For investors in the 47 per cent marginal tax rate*

After-tax return on shares — average	6.8 %
After-tax return on shares — range	-11.4% to 24.4%
After-tax return on fixed interest	5.3%

♦ *For investors in the 15 per cent marginal tax rate*

After-tax return on shares — average	8.6%
After-tax return on shares — range	-8.8% to 34.2%
After-tax return on fixed interest	8.7%

Looking at the lower figures for superannuation funds the after-tax return on fixed interest of 8.7 per cent is slightly greater than the estimated after-tax return of 8.6 per cent from shares. As shares involve a higher risk, those figures suggest that in current conditions a wiser course may be to place most superannuation fund capital in fixed interest.

For those in the highest marginal tax group the average estimated after-tax return on shares of 6.8 per cent per annum is about one fifth above the fixed-interest figure of 5.3 per cent. Some investors may consider that margin is insufficient to compensate for the higher risk of shares which is illustrated by the wide range of results — especially when the average dividend yield of 4 per cent puts the market just out of Zone 4 and into Zone 3, (on the zone ranking system described earlier in this book). That would suggest that results may be lower than average. So there would be a case for deferring substantial investment in shares until there were a more positive relationship between dividend yields and interest rates.

◆ *Information on share market*

In the Annex to Appendix A, there is a copy of page 3 of the February issue of the newsletter. The format of this page was designed to include significant information most of which is not available elsewhere. The chart, which shows only major turning points to emphasise medium and long term changes, includes the long term trend and upper and lower limits of the normal trading range. That concept is described in Chapter Eleven.

One glance at that chart is sufficient to show that investors at that time would have had serious reservations about widely publicised claims that the market had bottomed out. It is another reminder that decisions should be based on an objective examination, rather than accepting illogical claims based on looking only at the movements of the last year or so. There is no logic in suggesting that the market has bottomed out and a significant rise is imminent, just because it is about 20 per cent below the February 1994 peak and about the same amount below the peak of the most frantic boom of the century in 1987.

That page explains how the growth in dividend receipts and the effect of the tax credit are taken into account. Also included on that page in each issue are the average dividend yield and adjusted yield, the income handicap compared with medium term interest rate, the amount by which the All Ordinaries is above or below the long term trend, the downside risk if the market plunges below the trend as it did in 1974 and 1982, a brief comment on current market mood as well as certain other key index figures.

On page 2 in each issue are recommendations on current strategy. Each issue contains a page on fixed-interest investments including recommendations.

As an indication of the nature of the topics covered, the February 1995 issue included articles on the lessons from my 40 years investment experience, comments of value to investors in a book published 150 years ago and recent forewords to that book, a survey of the Westpac ADF *December protected*, the need for super fund trustees to be aware of a strategy for members close to retirement, the importance of price as well as other attractive features in selecting stocks, the reality of rises in house values as distinct from comments by advisers and writers, a discussion of the pros and cons of investing overseas.

There were also brief comments on allocated pensions and successful action by aggrieved investors in actions to recover from advisers losses they had suffered due to the failure of advisers to disclose all relevant facts to them.

Donnelly's Investing Today is published eight times a year. The March and September issues are accompanied by a supplement containing up-to-date comments on about 30 different types of investment products. At the time of writing in March 1995 the current subscription is $80 a year. See request for services form at the end of this book.

Index

A

B

Books written by Austin Donnelly

Investing

More Wealth With Less Risk — investing in the volatile 1990's	1993
More Wealth Through Beating the Money traps	1991
More Wealth With Less Risk	1990
The Three R's of Investing Second Edition	1987
The Three R's of Investing (Aust. version)	1985
Australian Investment Planning Guide	1985
The Three R's of Investing (US version)	1985
Where to Park Your Cash	1983
Seven Steps to Investing Success	1975
Investing for Profit in the 70's	1975
Strategic Investing	1973
Investing	1971
Successful Investment in Industrial & Mining Shares	1970
Investing for Profit	1969
How to Make Money in Investments ("Bullen Bear")	1967

Personal money management

Planning & Financing a Secure Retirement	1980
Personal Money Management	1979
You & Your Money in Australia	1966

Financial management

How to Generate & Control Cash Flow	1982
Treasury Management	1981
Managing Cash Flow	1979
Practical Financial Management	1978
Financial Management Second Edition	1964
Financial Management	1959

Management, accounting, business communication

Managing Meetings, Procedures & Chairmanship	1986
Successful Communication & Negotiation	1977
How to Make your Association Prosper	1966
Profit Through Cost Analysis & Direct Costing	1965
The Executive's Private Secretary	1963
Australian Secretarial Practice, Second Edition	1961
The Practice of Public Accounting, Second Edition	1961
Communication in Modern Business	1960
Trends in Public Accounting Practice	1956
Profitable Business Writing	1956
Guide to Business Management	1956
Secretarial Practice 1958	1958
Direct Costing 1957	1956
The Practice of Public Accounting	1953

Request for Services

To: Austin Donnelly, PO Box 5, Graceville East, Qld 4075.
Ph: (07) 892 4848 Fax: (07) 892 3744

Investment Advice

❑ I would like to obtain advice on investment or financial planning which is offered by Donnelly Money Management Pty Ltd from the Melbourne or Brisbane offices or by correspondence. I understand that the advice is offered on a fully professional, time-based fee system with all commissions received being passed on to the client. I also understand the basis on which the services are offered meet the standards of the Australian Investors Association.

Newsletter

❑ I wish to subscribe to *Donnelly's Investing Today*, annual subscription of $80.00.

More Wealth Through Beating the Money Traps

❑ Please supply ..... copy/copies of this book at $20.00 plus $3.00 postage and packing — total $23.00.

Recovery of Losses from Advisers and Fund Managers

❑ Please give me details of how you may be able to help me recover losses suffered as the result of investment advisers or fund managers failing to inform me of the full details of market risk and other factors of relevant investments.

Australian Investors Association

❑ I am interested in the Australian Investors Association. Please send details and membership application forms.

Name...Ph:...........................

Address..

....Code..........................

Enclosed is a cheque for $.......................or please debit my Visa/ Bankcard/Mastercard No:

❑❑❑❑ ❑❑❑❑ ❑❑❑❑ ❑❑❑❑

Expiry date: .... Signature................................

Please photocopy and send this page from the book.